Sandy Eis  g Sasso

MIDRASH

Reading the Bible with Question Marks

Afterword by Joan Chittister

PARACLETE PRESS
BREWSTER, MASSACHUSETTS

2017 Second Printing This Edition
2013 First Printing This Edition
2007 First Printing Hardcover Edition

Midrash: Reading the Bible with Question Marks

Copyright © 2007 by Sandy Eisenberg Sasso

ISBN 978-1-61261-416-8

Originally published in hardcover as *God's Echo: Exploring the Bible with Midrash*.

Translations: Throughout the book various biblical translations have been consulted, primarily *Tanakh: The Holy Scriptures—The New JPS Translation According to the Traditional Hebrew Text*, copyright 1985 by the Jewish Publication Society; and Robert Alter's *Genesis* (New York: W.W. Norton and Company, 1996). For both of these texts: All rights reserved; used by permission. In many cases the translation is the author's own.

    The Soncino Talmud, translated under the editorship of Rabbi Dr. I. Epstein (London: Soncino Press, 1978), has been used for Talmudic translations. Translations of midrashim are adapted from *Pesikta De-Rab Kahana*, translated from Hebrew and Aramaic by Willima G. Braude and Israel J. Kapstein (Philadelphia: Jewish Publication Society, 1975); *Midrash Rabbah* (10 volumes), edited by Dr. H. Freedman and Maurice Simon (New York: Soncino Press, 1983); and *The Midrash on Psalms* (volumes 1 and 2), translated from the Hebrew and Aramaic by William G. Braude (New Haven: Yale University Press, 1959).

The Paraclete Press name and logo (dove on cross) are trademarks of Paraclete Press, Inc.

The Library of Congress has catalogued the hardcover edition of this book as follows:
Sasso, Sandy Eisenberg.
  God's echo : exploring Scripture with midrash / Sandy Eisenberg
Sasso ; afterword by Joan Chittister.
    p. cm.
  ISBN 978-1-55725-478-8
  1. Bible. O.T. Pentateuch—Criticism, interpretation, etc.
  2. Midrash. 3. God (Judaism) I. Title.
BS1225.52.S29 2007
296.1'406—dc22   2007006829

10 9 8 7 6 5 4 3 2

Published by Paraclete Press
Brewster, Massachusetts
www.paracletepress.com

Printed in the United States of America

CONTENTS

For My Grandson, Darwin,
God's Echo

Part One

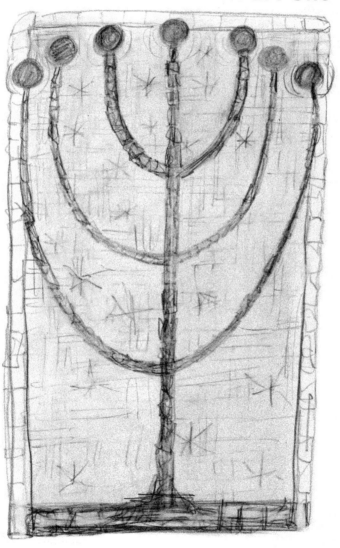

Is God Speaking to Me?
Listening to God's Echo

Customarily, when we read the Bible we listen to its ancient words, allowing it to tell us our ancestors' stories. But what would it mean to read the Bible by allowing it to help us tell the stories of *our* lives? What if we read our joys, our fears, and our doubts into the biblical narrative?

Then God's question to Adam and Eve after they have eaten the forbidden fruit in the Garden of Eden—"Where are you?"—would become a question for us, for now. What are we doing in our lives at this moment? Are we ashamed? Are we hiding from something, from someone? Are we running away? What part of Adam and Eve's story is our own? Asking such questions is the beginning of midrash.

If we approached Scripture in light of our own stories, all the stories of the Bible would read differently. Consider Esau sitting by his father's bedside, knowing that the blessing of the firstborn has been given to his younger brother, Jacob. Esau asks, "Father, have you only one blessing?" This is not simply a son's poignant plea to his father, Isaac, about the birthright. When we use midrash, Esau's question becomes a question for all

Note to the reader

You will see references such as this one—*Pesikta de-Rab Kahana* 12:25—throughout this book. *Midrashim* (the plural of *midrash*) are classic texts, and these are bibliographic references that make it possible for anyone to go back to the original sources.

Midrash, capitalized, refers to the classic written collections of the first millennium CE. I use *midrash*, lower case, as a generic reference.

of us who have ever felt rejected, cheated, or betrayed. We may ask ourselves, and the text itself: What part of Esau's life is like our own?

Rabbi Levi once commented on words from Exodus 20:2, "I am the Lord your God." He taught: "The Holy One appeared to the people as a statue with faces on every side, so that though a thousand people might be looking at the statue, they would be led to believe that it was looking at each one of them. So, too, when the Holy One spoke, each and every person in Israel could say, 'The Divine Word is addressing me'" (*Pesikta de-Rab Kahana* 12:25).

Listening to God's echo in our lives, approaching Scripture as if God were speaking to us, is the beginning of midrash.

The ancient Jewish sages following the biblical period were known as rabbis. They believed that the Word spoke to every generation anew. They allowed the biblical stories into their lives, and they let their lives enter the stories. They created midrash, interpretations of Scripture, an imaginative body of literature, which enriched the biblical narrative and kept it fresh and vital.

This book invites you to listen to some of the most beautiful selections of midrash, to hear how the words of Scripture spoke to others before us and influenced generations to this day. And then it invites you to do one thing more—to hear how the Word is still speaking to you.

What Is Midrash?

Reading the Bible with Question Marks

In the Bible story of the first murder, Cain kills his brother Abel. The biblical narrative says, "Cain said to his brother Abel . . . and when they were in the field Cain killed his brother Abel" (Genesis 4:8).

In the original Hebrew, the text does not tell us what Cain said to Abel. The conversation, or more likely the argument between the two brothers, is missing from the narrative. We are left wondering about the nature of the conflict that brought death and violence into the world.

The rabbis, writing between 400 and 1200 CE, filled in the gaps through midrash. Grounding themselves in the biblical narrative, they retold the ancient story in light of new realities and changing conditions. Through this interpretive method they made sense of contradictions in the text, provided missing information, and made the narrative relevant to the times in which they were living. Reading midrash allows us to become more familiar with the values, problems, and theology of another generation and invites us to consider how we too might add our own voices to the biblical text so that it continues to speak to our own generation.

Whereas modern biblical scholarship sees the Bible as a human document, written and edited in various stages, the rabbis assumed that the Torah was divinely revealed and therefore contained eternal, perfect truths, both evident and hidden meanings that required ongoing elucidation. The rest of the books of the Bible, what Jewish tradition refers to as Nevi'im, the Prophets, and Ketuvim, the Writings, were also considered products of divine inspiration.

Midrash does not challenge the idea that the Bible is divinely inspired or revealed. In fact, the rabbis believed that nothing in the Bible, not the choice of words or their spellings, not the order of events or the relationship of one text to another, was haphazard or inconsequential. Everything was intentional and purposeful. The rabbis deemed it their responsibility to discover connections and harmony where on the surface none appeared to exist. They believed it was possible for one text to contain multiple meanings. Chronology, as we understand it, was of no consequence. The rabbis felt free to read back into the patriarchal stories events that happened at the time of the Temple or, on the other hand, to see in the early stories of Genesis a foreshadowing of future events.

According to rabbinic thought, there are two Torahs, the Written Torah and the Oral Torah. The Written Torah is the biblical text (particularly the Pentateuch

Eventually, in about 200 CE, this Oral Torah was written down, edited, and compiled into a collection called the Mishnah. The Mishnah consists of six sections or orders divided into sixty-three tractates, each one further subdivided into chapters and paragraphs. When mishnaic references are included in this book, they indicate the tractate, chapter, and paragraph (e.g., Avot 1:1).

In the course of time a commentary to the Mishna, known as the Gemara, was written. Together the Mishna and the Gemara are called the Talmud. There are two Talmuds, one produced in Palestine and one in Babylonia, where many Jews were exiled after the destruction of the Temple in Jerusalem in 70 CE. The Palestinian Talmud was completed towards the end of the fourth century, and the Babylonian Talmud, which became the larger and more important in the life of the people, was completed in 500 CE. When quoting a passage from the Talmud, it is customary to cite the name of the tractate preceded by PT (Palestinian Talmud) or BT (Babylonian Talmud), followed by the number of the page and the letter "a" or "b," indicating the side of the page or folio quoted (e.g., BT Menahot 29b).

❉ ❉ ❉

or Five Books of Moses) as we have it. The Oral Torah is the interpretation that grew from Scripture and was eventually codified in a variety of texts, such as the Mishnah, the Talmud, and the Midrash. Rabbinic tradition teaches that God gave not only the Written but also the Oral Torah to Moses at Mount Sinai. It may be that the rabbis understood the Oral Torah to be their way of discovering meanings implicit in the text, allowing them to uncover what was already there, what was God's unspoken, original intent. Or it may be that they saw themselves deriving new meanings from the text, creating something new but rooted in tradition, and that ongoing human interpretation was indeed God's original intent.

* * *

Hasidism, a tradition beginning in the eighteenth century that popularized Jewish mystical teaching, taught that revelation was not a once-and-for-all event. The modern philosopher Martin Buber once wrote, "Everyone of Israel is told to think of himself as standing at Mount Sinai to receive the Torah. For man there are past and future events, but not so for God: day in and day out, He gives the Torah."[1]

A wonderful story in the Talmud illustrates this ongoing nature of revelation and the human responsibility for interpretation of Torah:

When Moses ascended Mt. Sinai, he found that God was attaching little crowns or decorations to the letters of the Torah. [In a Torah scroll, some of the Hebrew letters have ornamentations or crowns.] Moses asked God about the meaning of those decorations. God explained to Moses that someday in the future, a man would appear, named Akiba ben Joseph, who would be able to interpret the significance of the crowns. Moses asked God to allow him to meet this great teacher. God transported Moses [1200 BCE] through time, and brought him to the academy of Rabbi Akiba ben Joseph [second century CE].

Moses sat in the back of the classroom and listened to Akiba expound on the teachings of the Torah. Moses was distraught when he was unable to understand much of what Akiba was teaching.

When a certain subject was presented, the students asked Akiba, "How do you know this?" And Akiba responded, "This is a teaching from Moses on Sinai." And Moses was pleased. (BT Menahot 29b).

This Talmudic text may simply indicate that Akiba was such an extraordinary individual that he was capable of understanding something of God's Word, of Torah, that Moses in his time was not ready to grasp.

On the other hand, the rabbis may be suggesting that the Torah as received by the generation of Moses was not meant to be the last word. What Moses delivered amidst the thunder and lightning of Sinai was not a final product but rather the beginning of a conversation between God and the people of Israel. Revelation did not end with Moses but began with him. Torah as received by Moses was God's first word, and subsequent generations were to see themselves, like their ancestors, as also standing at the foot of Sinai receiving Torah. What Akiba taught, although incomprehensible to Moses, was nevertheless in the tradition of Moses, who began the process of interpreting God's Word.

Viewed in this light, the rabbinic passage about Akiba's classroom highlights the sacred nature of the ongoing process of interpretation that ensures the continuity of Torah through the generations. The crowns above the Hebrew letters, the rabbis are telling us, point to God's intention that the Torah text be interpreted.

In other Talmudic passages, the rabbis highlight Torah as a continuing revelation, and they underscore the divine desire to place the understanding and meaning of the Bible into the hands of its interpreters. The following rabbinic tale illustrates the importance of this process of human interpretation:

There was once a discussion in the academy concerning a matter of law. The rabbis differed as to the correct interpretation. Rabbi Eliezer offered every proof imaginable in order to support his position but still the other rabbis would not listen to him.

Rabbi Eliezer said to them, "If the law is according to me, let this carob tree prove it." And the carob tree moved a hundred cubits. Some say that the tree moved as much as four hundred cubits!

The other rabbis were not impressed and responded, "We don't learn proofs from a carob tree."

Then Rabbi Eliezer said to his colleagues, "If I am correct regarding this matter of law, then let this stream of water prove it." At that moment the stream of water turned and flowed backwards.

His colleagues said to him, "We don't learn proof for a matter of law from a stream of water."

Then Rabbi Eliezer proclaimed, "If the law is according to me, let the walls of the House of Study prove it." Just as he spoke the walls of the House of Study began to topple. But Rabbi Joshua rebuked the walls, saying, "When scholars are arguing about a matter of law, what business do you have to interfere in the conflict?" In honor of Rabbi Joshua the walls of the House of Study did not fall completely, but to honor Rabbi Eliezer, they did not become upright, but remained inclined.

Rabbi Eliezer then called upon Heaven to demonstrate the correctness of his position. He said, "If the law is according to me, then let the heavens prove it."

At that moment a Heavenly Voice cried out to all those assembled, "Why do you argue with Rabbi Eliezer? The law agrees with him in every case."

At that moment, Rabbi Joshua rose to his feet and exclaimed: *It is not in heaven* [Deuteronomy 30:1].

What did Rabbi Joshua mean by quoting this verse from Deuteronomy, *It is not in heaven*? Rabbi Jeremiah explained, "The Torah has already been given at Mount Sinai; we no longer pay attention to voices from heaven. Long ago You [God] wrote in the Torah at Mount Sinai, *After the majority must one incline*" [Exodus 23:2].

Some time later Elijah appeared to Rabbi Nathan, and the rabbi asked him what God did at that moment. Elijah said to him, "God laughed saying, 'My children have triumphed, my children have triumphed.'" (BT Bava Metzia 59b)

Not only the written words in the text, but the very process of interpreting those words, is divine. Despite the fact that Rabbi Eliezer was a well-known scholar who attracted many students and conducted his own academy, he could not claim to know what God had meant in a particular matter of law. Miracles were not acceptable as proof.

The authoritative textual understanding is "not in heaven" but with its earthly interpreters. God delights in the human imagination. No one person can claim to hold the key to unlock what God intended, because what God intended was for each generation to read its story into the text. In fact, the Torah itself teaches this: "Surely this Teaching which I enjoin you this day is not . . . beyond your reach. It is not in the heaven . . . neither is it beyond the sea. . . . No, the thing is very close to your mouth and in your heart, to observe it" (Deuteronomy 30:11–14).

In the Mishnah, we read the teaching of Ben Bag Bag concerning Torah: "Turn it and turn it again, for all is in it, and contemplate it, and grow gray and old over it, and stir not from it, for you can have no better rule than this" (Avot 5:26). These sources point away from a fundamentalist, literalist reading of the biblical text.

A Hasidic rabbi, Rabbi Mendel of Rymanov, offers the striking suggestion that what was heard on Mount Sinai was not the Ten Commandments but only the first letter of the first word of the first commandment. That Hebrew letter is *aleph* and it is silent—or, more precisely, it is the very beginning of sound. You open your mouth ready to speak. That is the *aleph*. Revelation here is not understood as containing specific content but as the very beginning of a conversation with God, a conversation in which we are all called to participate.

Burt Visotzky, a professor of midrash and interreligious studies, suggests that for the Bible to become more than an revered ancient book, but an eternal one that continues to speak to each new generation of readers, it must be open to interpretation:

> It is only in the reading and the rereading which each community does together that the Bible becomes a timeless text, the Word of God. . . . The give and take of interpretation creates an extra voice in the room, the sound of Reading the Book. When that happens, the Bible speaks not only to each community of readers, be they Jewish, Christian or any other flavor, but to all humanity.[2]

Robert Alter, a professor of Hebrew and comparative literature, likewise reminds us that by taking the Bible literally we miss its deeper meaning:

> Religious tradition has by and large encouraged us to take the Bible seriously rather than to enjoy it, but the paradoxical truth of the matter may well be that by learning to enjoy the biblical stories more fully as stories, we shall also come to see more clearly what they mean to tell us about

God, man, and the perilously momentous realm of history.[3]

New Testament scholar Raymond Brown made the same claim about understanding the Christian Scripture:

In Christian faith God's action climaxed in Jesus Christ who is once for all time (Heb. 10:10) so that after the gift of the divine Son no further revelation is needed—whence the theological axiom that revelation closed with the death of the last apostle. Yet there is no reason to think that God ceased to guide a developing interpretation of that action. Indeed, the subsequent role of the Spirit in human history, in the history of the church and its pronouncements, in the writings of the Fathers and theologians enters into *a Tradition that embodies the post-scriptural interpretation of the salvific action of God described in Scripture.* . . . People have continued finding in the NT meaning for their own lives as they face new issues; they have asked what the NT books mean, not simply what they meant. . . . Once a work is written, it enters into dialogue with its readers, including future readers. . . . The text is not simply an object on which the interpreter works analytically to extract a permanently univocal meaning; it is a structure that is engaged by readers in the process of achieving meaning and is therefore open to more than one valid meaning. Once written, a text is no longer under the author's control and can never be interpreted twice from the same situation.[4]

Amos Oz, a renowned Israeli author, once remarked, "Fundamentalists live life with an exclamation point. I prefer to live my life with a question mark." The rabbis turned the text and turned it again. They delighted in reading the Bible with question marks to discover not just what the Bible meant but what it continues to mean. They entered into dialogue with the text and added another voice in the room. And it was from these voices and question marks that they wrote midrashim.

Some historical background

In order to appreciate the environment in which midrash flourished, it is necessary to understand Jewish life in the early centuries of the Common Era. During most of the first century CE, Judaism was socially, politically, and religiously diverse. Many different groups populated the spiritual landscape. The Sadducees were the priests who administered the Temple in Jerusalem. Descendants of the high priest Aaron, they belonged to the upper social classes. The Sadducees constituted a hereditary group who interpreted the Bible literally.

According to the Bible, the Temple was first built by King Solomon, in about 1000 BCE. It was destroyed by the Babylonians (586 BCE), subsequently restored during Persian rule (515 BCE), and then renovated and expanded during the rule of Herod the Great (20 BCE). Built and rebuilt in the heart of Jerusalem, the Temple was the center of Jewish life until its destruction by the Romans in 70 CE. Its remains are now located in the Old City of Jerusalem.

* * *

The Pharisees came from the middle class and achieved their position of leadership by virtue of their learning, piety, and charisma. They understood themselves to be the successors of Moses, to whom God had entrusted the Torah at Sinai. The Pharisees took a more lenient approach to the Bible, interpreting Scripture and developing an Oral Torah alongside the Written Torah.

Other groups such as the Essenes, who preached an ascetic lifestyle in anticipation of the end of days, and the Zealots, who espoused political rebellion to overthrow Roman rule, helped to make up this heterogeneous community. In addition, various messianic and apocalyptic movements that yearned for divine redemption were part of the Jewish community of Israel and the Diaspora.

By 70 CE, when the Romans destroyed the Temple, everything had shifted. The messianic movement that had come to center around Jesus of Nazareth eventually gave birth to Christianity. Many of the Essenes had secluded themselves in a small area by the Dead Sea, Qumran, essentially withdrawing from society. The Zealots were defeated in their rebellion against Rome, and their political power was crushed. The priestly Sadducees lost their power base with the destruction of the Temple. It was left to one group, the Pharisees, to rescue the Jewish people from the political and spiritual catastrophe they had experienced and to ensure a Jewish future.

* * *

With the people exiled from their homeland and the Temple, which had served as the central sanctuary for sacrifice and worship, destroyed, the Jews yearned for a spiritual means to approach God. The Pharisees and their successors, the rabbis, secured Judaism's survival by teaching new ways of coming close to God through study, prayer, and deeds of loving-kindness. In place of the Temple, the rabbis elevated the home as a small sanctuary (*mikdash ma'at*) and established synagogues and academies as places of assembly, learning, and worship.

In those academies, the rabbis developed new ways of interpreting Scripture. They read the biblical text in light of the historical, political, and religious upheaval of their time, addressing the displacement and despair of their generation. These rabbis, the inheritors of the Pharisaic tradition, became the guardians of Torah.

Late in the first century CE in the city of Yavneh (or Jamnia), the rabbis engaged in the process of canonizing the Hebrew Bible, which came to be organized into three sections—Torah, Nevi'im (Prophets), and Ketuvim (Writings). The first letters for the Hebrew names for these divisions—T N K—give us the name for the Hebrew Bible, TaNaKh*. Most sacred of all the divisions was the Torah, which had been established since the time of Ezra.

---

* The vowels are provided for pronunciation. The K (*kaf*) at the end of a word is softened, hence kh.

In one of the most popular of the early rabbinic texts, we find the following line of succession:

Moses received the Torah (from God) at Sinai. He transmitted it to Joshua, Joshua to the Elders, the Elders to the Prophets, and the Prophets to the members of the Great Assembly. (Avot 1:1)

The priests are not included in this chain of tradition. Tractate Avot then continues to list the sayings or teachings of the early rabbinic sages who saw themselves as the successors to Moses and the authentic interpreters of Torah.

With the Temple lost and growing numbers of Jews living in exile from their land, the Bible—the TaNaKh—became, in the hands of these rabbis, a portable sanctuary, the spiritual homeland of the Jewish people. By dwelling in the text, by interpreting it and making it come alive, the people came to encounter the divine and continue a conversation begun long ago at Sinai.

Originally the teachings of the rabbis were only transmitted orally. The Mishnah became the first written collection of these teachings, followed by a supplement to or commentary on the Mishnah called the Gemara, created by later rabbinic teachers. Together, the Mishnah and the Gemara (words that

The Midrash is another large body of Jewish literature that developed during the first millennium CE. Unlike the Mishnah, which is topical, the biblical verse always serves as the starting point for the midrashic interpretation. While there are midrashim (plural of midrash) contained within the Talmud, there are also separate collections of midrashim that evolved over the centuries. In citing Midrash, references generally indicate the name of the midrashic collection, followed by chapter and paragraph (e.g., Genesis Rabbah 15:7).

In this book we will explore how the rabbis made meaning of the Bible through midrash, and we will discover how we might use this imaginative and creative method to allow the biblical text to speak to us.

both mean *teaching*) make up the Talmud. As noted above, there were two Talmuds, one produced in Palestine and one in Babylonia, where many Jews had been exiled after the First Temple's destruction. The Mishnah is the same in both Talmuds, but there are two versions of the Gemara, representing the Palestinian and Babylonian academies.

* * *

Product and process

Midrash is both a product—a body of literature written over a period of time, and a process—a way of interpreting sacred text that continues to the present day. In addressing questions about how to apply the Bible to new historical and social situations and how to find contemporary communal and personal meaning and significance in the Torah's ancestral legacy, the rabbis produced numerous collections of midrash. Those that concern exclusively legal matters are called Midrash Halachah. Those that focus on narrative and center on philosophical, moral, and historical questions are called Midrash Aggadah. We will focus primarily on the collections of Midrash Aggadah.

Exploring Midrash (the product), studying how the sages came to make sense and derive significance out of the ancient, sacred biblical text, opens us up to new appreciations of how tradition evolves and speaks through the generations. It is not possible to understand what it means to be a Jew without understanding how the rabbis interpret the Bible. Judaism wears a rabbinic lens in reading biblical text and living out its teachings. Just as Christians read the Hebrew Scripture through the eyes of the New Testament—which in some ways could be regarded as Christian midrash—so Jews read that Scripture through the eyes of the Talmud and Midrash and rabbinic commentaries.

Learning midrash (the process) is more than a fascinating historical excursus; it is a personal journey. My own encounters with midrash have helped give expression to my innermost longings, my deepest fears, and my most profound joys. I have marveled at how much of what the rabbis wrote still speaks to my concerns and moves my soul. Even more, I remain grateful for the tools they have provided to unlock new sacred treasures, how their imagination enables me to go deeper into my own.

I recall teaching a class in midrash to a group of adult women at my congregation. After exploring numerous midrashic texts, I invited the class to imagine what the text might mean to them. I asked them to add their own voices to the biblical narrative, using the process of midrash with which they had become familiar. Most of the participants were reluctant. One woman expressed the group's apprehension by saying, "I didn't know we, in our generation, could do that."

Midrash gives us permission to do just that, not only to be descendants but to become ancestors who bequeath our spiritual quest to future generations. We approach this task with a deep sense of humility, honoring its ancient origins and layers upon layers of understandings. After all, who are we, tied as we are to our own time and place, to attempt to fashion sacred words out of our distress and dreams? And yet, the authors of the Midrash ask, who are we, bearers of the image of God, not to pour our souls into the crucible of time, to affix our names to the holy narrative?

Learning midrash, the product and the process, enabled one woman in my congregation whose husband was a quadriplegic and was undergoing serious surgery, to pour out her soul into the story of the binding of Isaac. This story is read in the synagogue each year on the holy day of Rosh Hashanah, the Jewish New Year. The woman's words give new meaning to a difficult narrative.

Each year as the Jewish New Year approaches, I wonder why it was decided by the rabbis that we should read the story from Genesis about Abraham and his family. I believe it is to remind us that each of us climbs a mountain, as Abraham climbs Mount Moriah, sometimes individually, sometimes with others, but always alone. Though we never know what is at the top until we get there, I think the story is God's way of reminding us that the ram is always there. And God is always there.

I sat in the hospital room not knowing for sure what the results of the surgery would be. I held on to that faith that Abraham had when he climbed that mountain with Isaac, not knowing what was going to happen or how it was going to all turn out. But he had faith and that gave him strength to get past that moment, to believe in the best outcome. I wasn't denying that things could go wrong or that the outcome might be different from my best prayers. It was just believing in the presence of that other power and gaining strength from that belief.

Perhaps the reason for reading the story of Abraham and Isaac at the beginning of the Jewish New Year is not to remind us of Abraham or Isaac but to remind us of the mountain—the journey. When I really began to look into the different thoughts on the story, I began to realize how different each person's journey is. Isaac's journey was not the same as Abraham's; his was not the same as Sarah's; and the servants who accompanied them had an even different experience. They made the journey together, and yet separately.

We read the story together. All ears listen to the same words, perhaps hearing different things, but we are all together in the reading. So really we aren't alone as we climb. I have learned that during this crisis in my life. Just as Abraham had his servants waiting for him, there are many hearts and hands waiting for us, ready to help.

(From a letter written by Sue Baker, member of Congregation Beth El Zedeck, Indianapolis, Indiana, 2006)

We may all read the same words of the Bible, but we hear with different ears, depending on our religious traditions, our personal experiences, and our needs. Midrash invites us to be attuned to the many sounds that the text makes in our souls. A nineteenth-century Hasidic rabbi, Nachman of Breslov, once said, "Two men who live in different places, or even in different generations, may still converse. For one may raise a question, and the other who is far away in time or space may make a comment or ask a question that answers it."

The following chapters invite you to participate in a conversation with the rabbinic sages of old. You may agree, argue, or debate with them. Their imagination may perplex you or excite you. Their questions may trouble you or uplift you. I hope their interpretation will encourage you to listen more deeply not only to the ancient sacred story but also to the story that resonates within you and is waiting to be told.

A fourfold method

But first, let us look briefly at the fourfold method of interpretation used by the rabbis in ancient midrash. The same principles may guide us today.

The rabbis interpret the verse from Jeremiah, "Is not My word like . . . a hammer that breaks the rock into pieces?" (Jeremiah 23:29), by saying: "As the hammer splits the rock into many splinters, so will a scriptural verse yield many meanings" (BT Sanhedrin 34a). One text is not intended to have a single interpretation but is meant to yield different meanings depending on the readers, their generation, and their life experiences.

Often, without even realizing it, we read biblical narratives through the eyes of their interpreters. For example, most people assume that the fruit of the tree of knowledge of good and evil that Adam and Eve ate was an apple. It is so described in literature and depicted in art. But the text tells us nothing about the type of fruit. Genesis 3:6 simply states, "When the woman saw that the tree was good for eating and a delight to the eyes, and that the tree was desirable as a source of wisdom, she took its fruit and ate. She also gave some to her husband, and he ate."

The rabbis disagree as to what was the fruit of the tree. One rabbi suggests that Adam and Eve ate wheat, imagining that in the Garden of Eden wheat stalks grew like the cedars of Lebanon. Another rabbi says that Adam and Eve ate grapes. Still another identifies the fruit with an etrog, or citron. One interpreter states that the fruit must have been a fig, since only the fig tree offered its leaves to clothe Adam and Eve. Some believed that the nature of the fruit was purposely hidden in order to protect its honor, so no one could say that through this particular tree death was brought into the world (Genesis Rabbah 15:7).

The rabbis employed four different methods for interpreting passages such as these. By examining each of them and applying them to a scriptural verse, we can better appreciate the meaning of midrash. Consider, for instance, these words from the Exodus, chapter two, verse five: "The daughter of Pharaoh came down to bathe in the Nile, while her maidens walked along the Nile. She spied the basket among the reeds and sent her slave girl to fetch it."

The first method of interpretation involves observing the most straightforward meaning of the passage. This is called *peshat,* which is the Hebrew word for plain or simple. It is nothing other than noting the details of the verse—who are the characters, what happens, in what order. In the Exodus passage, we learn that the daughter of Egypt's highest ruler came with her servants to wash herself in the river Nile. She saw a basket floating in the river and sent a servant to bring it to her.

The second level of interpretation looks for connections between one text and another. Sometimes the rabbis see an allegorical meaning in the passage or recognize that the text is hinting at something other than what appears in its plain meaning. This is called *remez*. In the Exodus verse about Pharaoh's daughter, we notice that the Hebrew word for basket (*teva*) is the same as the Hebrew word for ark in the Noah story of Genesis. There is a connection, then, between the vessel that carried Noah and the one that carried Moses. Even as Noah's "ark" saved humanity from complete destruction, the "ark" that saved Moses made possible the redemption of the people of Israel. The story of saving Israel is related to the story of saving the world. The ark (*teva*) is a symbol of salvation.

The third method of understanding Scripture is called *drash,* or midrash. The word means "to search out," and midrash seeks to derive a homiletical meaning from the passage. It is a way of reading into the text what may not be immediately apparent. In the verse about Pharaoh's daughter, the rabbis wonder why a princess, the daughter of Pharaoh, would need to leave the luxury and comfort of the palace to go down to the Nile to bathe. After all, she could have had her servants bring her the water she needed to wash herself. The midrash says that Pharaoh's daughter went to the Nile to cleanse herself of her father's idolatry.

In another chapter, we will discuss in further detail the midrashim surrounding this passage, but suffice it for now to say that the rabbis, in interpreting the text in this way, are seeking to fill in what appears to be missing from the Exodus narrative about the character of the Egyptian woman who becomes the instrument for redeeming the people of Israel. Nothing in the passage hints at this, but the rabbis imagine a woman who distinguishes herself from the rest of Egypt's leaders.

The fourth method of interpretation is called *sod*, or secret. It is the mystical understanding of the biblical narrative. A vast literature of mysticism (later known as Kabbalah) developed in Judaism from the time of the destruction of the Second Temple through the present day. Torah was interpreted according to a highly symbolic system that revealed the mysteries of the heavens and of God. The words of Scripture were understood to contain hidden meanings that revealed not just the life of human beings in their search for God, but also the inner nature of the divine.

The mystical, or *sod*, understanding of Pharaoh's daughter is radically different from the other interpretations we have encountered. Pharaoh's daughter symbolizes the *Shekhinah*, God's indwelling presence. When she sees the weeping child who represents Israel, she is roused to compassion.

The passage refers to mystical teachings that see oppression and evil as a result of the imbalance in the universe between absolute justice and compassion. Only when strict judgment and loving-kindness are in harmony is redemption possible. The fourth level of interpretation shows that the passage about Pharaoh's daughter is much more than what it seems. It is not just referring to the earthly concerns of redemption from Egyptian bondage but is alluding to heavenly matters, the very inner workings of the divine.

If we take the first letter of each method of interpretation—*peshat, drash, remez,* and *sod*—and add vowels, we form the word *pardes*, which means "orchard." The symbolism is rich: as an orchard provides shade and sweet fruit for those who enter, so it receives the care and nurture of those who come to enjoy its produce. There is mutual relationship and mutual benefit. In the same way, the Torah gives shade and sustenance to those who read it, while those who read and interpret Scripture are like those who tend the orchard, nourishing Torah.

Part Two

How Does Midrash Speak to Us?
Listening to Your Story

Over the years I have read and taught many midrashim. I have always been amazed at how at one point in my life a particular midrash seems interesting simply as a piece of classical rabbinic literature, while at another it appears to speak out of the ages directly to me. Life changes you, and what at one time is someone else's narrative becomes your own, one you were meant to retell.

The midrashim in the following section are those I have felt are part of my story, ones I was meant to retell. They talk about rejection and anger and the blessing of healing and repentance. Just when I have thought forgiveness was unattainable, when even the ancient rabbis seemed to despair of human nature and the world, their writings offered me the surprising promise of a new beginning.

The selections in the next pages are more than just ancient narratives. They speak not only in the past, but in the present tense. They help us unwrap treasures of hope, courage, and faith.

Each chapter begins with a biblical verse on which the rabbis base their midrash. Following the classical midrashic text, we will look at the meaning of the rabbinic interpretation, at how the rabbis read their lives into the Bible. The reflections at the end of each chapter are my own personal encounters with midrash. They and the questions that follow are an invitation for you to hear how the sacred words are still speaking to you.

In the following midrashim, the rabbis address many of the questions with which I have struggled. I recall at an especially difficult time saying, "If this is what God intends, then I don't believe in God." At that moment my daughter reminded me, "Mom, but you don't believe in that kind of God." Midrash has helped me explore the question that remained—in what kind of God do I believe? I hope it will help you in your faith journey as well.

Revelation Takes Place All the Time
Looking into God's Mirror

The rabbis said that when God revealed the Ten Commandments at Sinai, not only the Exodus generation stood at the foot of the mountain, but all generations of Israel yet to come. They believed that revelation did not take place once upon a time but all the time.

Moses heard God not only amidst the thunder and lightning on top of a mountain, but in the quiet of the desert before a lowly thorn bush. When I ask people to tell me about those places in their lives where they feel God's presence, they speak of nature, neighborhood, and family. They mention blue spruces, bedsides, and dining tables.

One woman says, "I first became aware of the presence of God when sitting under a willow tree. I thought this couldn't be a mistake." Another speaks of the sacred in the center of a city, where people gather for fellowship. Still another finds the spirit at home rising like yeast left to rest in a warm kitchen. And as the breath of God that first blew atop a mountain now blows through each of them, they call God by different names.

* * * * * * * * * * * * * * * *

The biblical verses upon which the midrashim are based begin each midrash. Sometimes the rabbis refer to other verses in the midst of their commentaries. All Bible verses are in italics. The midrashim are in bold characters. Also, you will notice references to various rabbis throughout the midrashim. Below, for instance, we hear from Rabbi Levi as well as Rabbi Yose son of Rabbi Hanina. These were rabbis mostly from the Talmudic period whose teachings are preserved and transmitted by the editors of the Midrash.

The following midrashim are all related, and together they ask us to consider the divine blowing through our lives and the many names we call God.

THE MIDRASH

I am the Lord your God. (Exodus 20:2)

The voice of the Lord is in strength. (Psalm 29:4)

I am the Lord your God. . . . It is written, *Has a people ever heard the voice of God . . . ?* (Deuteronomy 4:33). . . . Rabbi Levi explained: Had it said "the voice of God is in His strength," the world would not have been able to survive, but it says instead: *The voice of God is in strength* (Psalm 29:4)—that is, according the strength of each individual, the young, the old, and the very small ones. God said to Israel: "Do not believe that there are many deities in heaven because you have heard many voices, but know that I alone am the Lord your God, as it says, *I am the Lord your God*" (Deuteronomy 5:6).

(Exodus Rabbah 29:1)

Another, related midrash:

I am the Lord your God. (Exodus 20:2)

Note that Scripture does not say, "I am the Lord your [plural] God," but *I am the Lord your [singular] God.*

Rabbi Yose son of Rabbi Hanina said: The divine Word spoke to each and every person according to his particular capacity [his strength] [Hebrew: *koho*]. And do not be surprised at this idea. For when manna came down to Israel, each and every person tasted it in keeping with his own capacity. . . . Thus for the infants . . . the manna tasted like mothers' milk. For it is said, *its taste was like the taste of rich cream* (Numbers 11:8); for the young it tasted like rich bread, for it is said, *the choice flour, the oil and the honey, which I had provided you to eat* (Ezekiel 16:19); and the old tasted the manna according to their capacity for it is said, *the taste of it was like wafers made with honey* (Exodus 16:31).

Now what was true about the manna was equally true about the divine Word. Each and every person heard it according to his own particular capacity [his strength]. Thus David said, *The voice of the Lord is in strength* (Psalm 29:4)—

**not "The voice of the Lord is in His strength,"
but the voice of the Lord is in the strength and
capacity of each and every person. Therefore the
Holy One said: "Do not be misled because you
hear many voices. Know that I am one and the
same: *I am the Lord your God.*"**
(Pesikta De-Rab Kahana 12:25)

In these first texts, the rabbis are asking what it might
be like to actually hear God's voice. They question
the ability of human beings to bear the enormous
power of direct divine speech. At the same time they
are struck by the many differing interpretations of the
divine Word.

The rabbis do not doubt the existence of one God, but
they are puzzled by the multiple ways in which people
understand revelation. If God speaks with one voice, how
is it possible for people to hear different things? Why is
there more than one understanding of revelation? Why
are there so many interpretations of Scripture?

Rabbi Levi suggests a possible explanation. Each
individual receives only what he or she is able to bear
or comprehend. God addresses all, young and old, even
children, but each hears with a different ear. God is like
an extraordinary orator who speaks to a large crowd of
people, and yet each listener walks away saying, "The
speaker was talking to me."

The second text further elaborates on this idea. The rabbis wonder why, if God is talking to a large multitude gathered at the foot of Mount Sinai, the biblical text uses the singular pronoun when it says, *I am the Lord your God*.

These midrashim offer a good example of finding theological significance in grammatical details. God is, in fact, talking directly to each individual. Each person hears and sees something unlike what others hear and see; each apprehends an aspect of God's presence, albeit not the whole. All depends on an individual's age, experience, and perspective.

So Rabbi Yose son of Rabbi Hanina understands the Hebrew word for strength to signify *capacity* or *ability*. When the biblical text says that "the voice of the Lord is in strength," it does not mean that God speaks through strong and powerful acts. If that were the intent of the passage, the verse would have read, "the voice of the Lord is in *His* strength." Instead the rabbi suggests that each individual hears God as he or she is able, in keeping with his or her capacity for understanding.

The midrash then draws on a number of other, seemingly unrelated biblical verses in reference to the manna that served as food for the people of Israel during their years of wandering in the desert. The manna had the extraordinary ability to provide what was necessary to sustain the entire community. It gave the nutrition of mother's milk to the infants, which was indispensable for their survival. It provided the sustenance of bread with the taste of thick cream to the young men, who craved a richer diet. It offered the necessary nourishment of soft wafers and sweet honey for the elderly, whose digestive systems required milder fare.

Just as God had provided manna for the people in the wilderness and yet it tasted different to each person, so did God reveal the divine Word to all who stood at Sinai; yet each person heard something different. The people heard what they needed at the moment to sustain them on their journey. It was as though each person left Sinai saying, "God was speaking to me."

Still another midrash, commenting on the verse from Exodus, "I am the Lord your God," focuses on how different historical experiences serve to shape each generation's way of perceiving the divine.

THE MIDRASH

The Holy One appeared to Israel at the Red Sea as a mighty person waging war and appeared to them at Sinai as a scribe who teaches Torah. . . . The Holy One said to Israel, "Do not be confused because you see Me in many guises, for I am the One who was with you at the Red Sea and at Sinai: *I am the Lord your God."*

(Pesikta De-Rab Kahana 12:24)

For a generation concerned with escaping bondage, God was the power that enabled the people to defeat the Egyptian army. For the individuals standing at the foot of Mount Sinai, God was the patient educator teaching a disparate group of people the laws and traditions that would bind them into a community. Another midrash suggests that when Moses first heard God speaking to him at the burning bush, it sounded like the voice of his father, Amram.

THE MIDRASH

God said, "I am the God of your father. . . ."
(Exodus 3:6)

Moses was a novice in prophecy; hence God thought: "If I reveal Myself to him in a loud voice,

I will terrify him, and if in a soft voice he will think lightly of prophecy." What did God do? God revealed Himself in the voice of his father.
  (Exodus Rabbah 3:1)

Moses hears what he is capable of hearing. The voice of God corresponds to the need and strength of Moses as he tends the flock of his father-in-law, Jethro. At that moment in his journey, Moses is lonely. He has fled Egypt after killing an Egyptian taskmaster. He has been exiled from Pharaoh's court, separated from the family he has only recently come to know as his own. He yearns for a familiar sound. When God speaks, what Moses hears is the sound of his father's voice calling to him. This is the one God, the God of Abraham, the God of Isaac, and the God of Jacob, but to Moses, the divine Word reverberates in his father's loving voice, calling him home. If he is to return to his people, to lead them out of bondage, this is the voice he desperately needs to hear.

The rabbis could have advanced the notion that there is only one definitive understanding of Scripture, but they did not. God's Word is too vast and encompassing to yield solely one meaning. While the rabbis would derive uniform laws to govern the community, they would delight in the multiplicity of textual interpretations. Consequently, it is possible to accept what might appear to be mutually exclusive explanations of the quarrel between Cain and Abel or the special blessing of the Sabbath, as we will see in subsequent chapters. And so the rabbis could say about two sages (Hillel and Shammai) who almost always disagreed with one another, "These and these are the words of the living God."

The rabbis ask: If both the House of Hillel and House of Shammai speak words of the living God, then why did the House of Hillel merit that the law be established according to their words? The Talmud offers the following reason: The sages of the House of Hillel were pleasant and modest, and they would teach their words and the words of the House of Shammai. Not only that, but they would mention the words of the House of Shammai before their own words (BT Eruvin 13b).

The rabbis emphasized the need to take each other's opinions seriously and to offer one's own with humility. What mattered was not just the cleverness and brilliance of a particular interpretation but the way in which it was shared, without ridicule or shame.[5]

If no one individual can bear to hear the direct and powerful divine voice, if all that is heard is refracted through the many who listen, then it is not possible to assume textual arrogance. What we know of God is what we need at that moment to sustain us on our journey, but it is only a partial knowing. Thus, the rabbis teach:

An individual produces many coins from one die, but they look alike. God, on the other hand, could stamp every individual with the die of the first human being, yet not one of them looks like the other.

(Sanhedrin 4:5)

The sages—and God—loved that sort of diversity. Since human beings are created in the image of God and no one looks like another, it is required to look in the faces of all people to catch a glimpse of the vastness of the divine. So individuals, from the very young to the very old, provide different insights into the divine Word. Likewise, it is necessary to take seriously all interpretations to begin to approximate the voice that is beyond hearing. One Word came from God as the people stood at Sinai, yet each of us is being addressed now, wherever we stand. One Word came from God, but it yielded (and continues to yield) many meanings.

A PERSONAL REFLECTION

I have always been struck by the Jewish teaching that God is like a mirror, and everyone who looks into it sees a different face. After all, Abraham, Isaac, and Jacob each looked into that mirror and saw different faces and so called God by different names. For Abraham, who went forth on a divine promise to become a great nation, God was Protector. Abraham's God was known as *Magen Avraham*, Shield of Abraham. For Isaac, who was bound to an altar and who only at the last moment was saved from his father's knife, God was Awesome One. Isaac's God was known as *Pachad Yitzhak*, Fear of Isaac. For Jacob, who left his home to travel to Haran, afraid of his brother's wrath and uncertain of the future, God was Mighty One. Jacob's God was known as *Avir Ya'akov*, the Power of Jacob. The rabbis attribute to Abraham, Isaac, and Jacob names for God that reflect the patriarchs' experience and understanding of the divine. Each naming was an appropriate name for God, but it was an incomplete apprehension, a partial knowing of the One who includes them all.

Jewish tradition teaches that there over one hundred names for God. Still we tend to limit the way we call on God to just a few names such as Father, King, or Lord. Yet if, as the midrash states, God speaks to each and every individual and each person hears as he or she is able, I wonder what would happen if each person would look directly into God's mirror. What would be his or her name for God?

I once asked a group of children to think of a favorite name for God. I suggested the traditional names and then offered others like Mother, Healer, and Friend. I recall a young boy about six years old whose mother had been battling breast cancer since he was only one year old. He raised his hand and when I called on him, without a moment's hesitation, he said, "My favorite name for God is Healer."

I decided to try a similar exercise with a group of adult women. I asked them to think about a name for God that best reflected the place where they were in their lives. I reminded them that there are many names for God, and that people throughout the generations have called God out of the depths of their souls. We studied the midrash about how at Sinai each person heard the Word differently, according to his or her capacity. I suggested that if we rely only on names of God or interpretations of Scripture that have little or nothing to do with our own life experiences, then we stop doing what our ancestors did, looking in God's mirror. I reminded them that they were not only descendants receiving the vast tradition of those who came before then, but also ancestors, who must pour their souls into the ancient narrative and allow it to speak afresh to another generation.

I noted that in the traditional midrash the rabbis mentioned infants, the young, and old men. The midrash imagined how the manna in the wilderness tasted to each group. And I wondered what it might have tasted like to young women and elderly women. I asked what the divine revelation might have sounded like to the women as they heard the words in keeping with their understanding.

We learned the one name for God given by a woman in the Bible. This is recorded in Genesis, when Hagar was sent into the wilderness pregnant with her son, Ishmael, and she despaired. Then an angel of God spoke to Hagar and revealed that her son's name would be Ishmael. At that moment, Hagar offered her name for God, *El Ro'i*, the One Who Sees Me (Genesis 16:13).

Our group spent some time talking, and then we agreed that each would find a quiet place to discover her own name for God. It took quite a while before anyone felt comfortable speaking her name for God aloud to the members of the group. For each of the women, this was the first time that anyone had asked them to look in God's mirror. After a long period of silence, names finally came. One woman said, "I would like to call God 'An Old Warm Bathrobe.'" Everyone present acknowledged and affirmed her naming, but I'll admit we thought it a little unusual.

I forgot about that experience until one year later. The same woman, whom I had not seen in twelve months, made a point of calling me and telling me how much that exercise meant to her. Her mother had died that past year, and she took her old warm bathrobe and wrapped it around her. She felt the presence of God.

WHERE DO YOU SEE YOURSELF IN THE STORY?

If you looked in God's mirror, what would you see? What is your name for God?

How is God speaking to you now, in the place in life where you are?

Remember a time when the way you saw or heard the divine in your life was different from now. What changed? What remained the same?

Should Humans Have Been Created?
Shaping the World out of Compassion

We only have to open the daily newspapers to find stories that tell us of the worst of human nature. Even as examples of murder, abuse, and dishonesty make the headlines, so on a smaller scale and in many personal ways we experience the hurt that one human being can visit upon another.

There are days when we are faced with so much of life's dark side that we are inclined to despair. At such moments in their own lives, the rabbis wondered whether creation was such a good thing. Witnessing all the cruelty and oppression, all the hurt and pain one person caused another, they asked the almost unthinkable question—should people have been created? Did humanity deserve the gift of life?

The unexpected question yielded an equally surprising answer. Perhaps it would have been better if human beings had not been created. The rabbis do not mask their disappointment in human failure. Yet they find in God's decision for creation, even with overwhelming evidence presented against it, the grace upon which the world is established and endures.

The following midrashim ask us to look fully in the face of evil and still to discover the powerful gifts of repentance and forgiveness that open us to see the grace in our own lives.

THE MIDRASH

Let us make the human in our image. . . . (Genesis 1:26)

Rabbi Hanina said that when God came to create Adam, God took counsel with the ministering angels, saying to them, *Let us make the human.* "What shall his character be?" asked the angels. God answered, "Righteous people shall spring from him," as it is written, *For the Lord knows the way of the righteous,* which means that the Lord made known the way of the righteous to the ministering angels; *But the way of the wicked shall perish* (Psalm 1:6): God hid this knowledge from them. Had God revealed to the angels that the wicked would spring from Adam, the quality of Justice would not have permitted humans to be created.

Rabbi Simon said: When the Holy One, the blessed One, came to create Adam, the ministering angels formed themselves into groups and parties, some of them saying, "Let the human be created," while others urged, "Let the human not

be created." Thus it is written, *Love and Truth fought together; righteousness and peace combated each other* (Psalm 85:11). Love said, "Let humans be created, because they will dispense acts of love"; Truth said, "Let humans not be created, because they will speak falsehood"; Righteousness said, "Let humans be created, because they will perform righteous deeds"; Peace said, "Let humans not be created, because they are full of strife." What did the Lord do? He took Truth and cast it to the ground. Said the ministering angels before the Holy One, "Sovereign of the Universe! Why do You despise Your seal? Let Truth arise from the earth!" Hence it is written, *Let truth spring up from the earth* (Psalm 85:12).

Rabbi Huna, the Elder of Sepphoris, said: While the ministering angels were arguing and disputing with each other, the Holy One, the blessed One, created humans. God said to the angels: "For what purpose do you argue? Humans have already been made!"

(Genesis Rabbah 8:4–5)

In this midrash the rabbis are attempting to address the question of what is meant by God saying, *Let us create.* . . . Shouldn't the verse have read: *Let me create . . .?*

While this is not a problem grammatically, since God often speaks in the royal "we," the midrash uses the plural to imagine a scenario where God consults the angels about the creation of humanity.

In the first part of the midrash, God argues for the creation of human beings by emphasizing their righteousness, quoting only half a biblical verse [Psalm 1:6] to the angels. God omits the second part of the verse that highlights the wicked side of human nature, for fear that the angels would object to the creation of man and woman.

In the second part of the midrash, Rabbi Simon imagines the angels arguing with one another. With a play on words, the midrash interprets Psalm 85:11 not as *righteousness and peace have kissed* [nashaku] *each other*, but as *righteousness and peace have combated* ["taken up weapons"—from the Hebrew *neshek* meaning weapon] *each other*. Thus, the angels contend: The Angel of Love favors the creation of human beings because humans will perform acts of loving-kindness. But the Angel of Truth objects, claiming that humans will tell lies. The Angel of Righteousness agrees with the Angel of Love because man and woman will perform good deeds. However, the Angel of Peace claims that humans are full of strife.

As it stands, the vote is two angels in favor, two against. God has to break the tie and does so by casting

Truth to the ground. It is not that the Angel of Truth is incorrect in assessing the human character. It is just that God so wants to create human beings that despite knowing that they will lie and contend with each other, God is willing to cast Truth aside.[6]

The angels take no comfort in God's decision. In one chorus they speak on behalf of their disregarded fellow angel, saying, "*Let truth spring up from the earth*," and return to its proper place in the heavens. But God pays no heed to the angels, for if Truth assumed its proper place in the heavens, humanity could not exist.

The Talmud records a similar debate between the academies of Hillel and Shammai, two of the most respected rabbis of the first century BCE, whose disciples continued to influence Jewish teaching for many generations: "For two years the disciples of these two great sages disagree about whether human beings should have been created." In the end, they conclude that it would have been better if people had not been created. But since they have already been created, let them be attentive to their deeds (BT Eruvin 13b).

The reader might have expected a different account by the rabbis. Such pessimism is surprising. The biblical text in Genesis had proclaimed that God deemed all of creation good. Yet the rabbis may be telling us something about the experience of their own generation, their own disappointments about creation and human nature.

The midrashim reflect both the historical strife of the period and the internal failings the rabbis saw within their community. In articulating the angels' debate, the rabbis are expressing their own.

The rabbis are not nihilistic. It is not that humans are a lost cause. After all, two angels stand in their defense. People can be loving, honorable, and upright. Moreover, there appears to be a divine purpose behind their creation. Despite wickedness, deceit, and war, God still cherishes human beings. In the end, it is God's compassion that assures the creation of humanity.

A midrash on Psalm 89 highlights the power of divine grace and compassion in sustaining the world:

THE MIDRASH

For I have said: the world is built on hesed *[mercy, lovingkindness]; in the very heavens you establish your faithfulness. . . .* (Psalm 89:3)

And not only the heavens, but also the throne of God is established on *hesed*, **as it is said,** *In* **hesed** *shall the throne be established"* **(Isaiah 16:5). To what may this be compared? To a person who sat on a throne that had four legs, one of which was short. . . . Therefore, he took a pebble and propped it up. So the throne in heaven was shaken until the Holy One, the blessed One**

propped it up. And with what did God prop it up? With mercy [*hesed*]. Hence it is said, "The world is built on mercy."

(Midrash Tehillim on Psalm 89:2)

The world is like a throne with four legs, one of which is too short to enable the throne to stand upright. God's creation is likewise precarious, constantly tottering between survival and extinction. Only *hesed*, mercy and divine grace, sustain its existence.

Many other midrashim similarly underscore the importance of divine compassion for rabbinic theology, seeing its presence even in the midst of human disobedience.

THE MIDRASH

Cain went out from the presence of the Lord.
(Genesis 4:16)

Rabbi Hanina ben Isaac said: He went forth rejoicing, as you read, *He goes forth to meet you, and when he sees you, he will be glad in his heart* (Exodus 4:14). Adam met Cain and asked, "What was done in punishment of you?" Cain replied, "I vowed repentance and was granted clemency." Upon hearing this, Adam, in self-reproach, began to beat his face as he said, "Such is the power of repentance, and I knew it not." Then and there

Adam exclaimed, *It is a good thing to confess* **[give thanks]** *to the Lord* **(Psalm 92:1).**
(Genesis Rabbah 22:12)

The rabbis understand the Genesis verse about Cain going out from the presence of God to mean that Cain went forth glad in heart. This seems improbable. Given the brutality of his deed of murder, Cain is not only banished from his home, destined to be a wanderer, but also apparently exiled from God. How could the midrash imagine him with a glad heart?

The midrash does not deny Cain's sin but imagines that God remains with him. While Cain must bear the consequences of his actions, he finds some relief in repentance. Cain's sin calls forth God's justice; Cain's regret arouses God's compassion.

Adam is amazed. He had no idea that atonement had such power. He reproaches himself for not repenting after eating from the Tree of Knowledge of Good and Evil. Would his world have been different had he done so? While the physical consequences of his act might have been the same, perhaps his psychological burden would have been lighter.

Atonement and forgiveness are themes that surface throughout the midrash. In Genesis (6:14), God commands Noah: *Make an ark of cedar wood.* The midrash reads:

Noah repented and planted trees of cedar. The people asked him, "Why these cedars?" Noah said to them, "The Holy One, the blessed One, is about to bring a flood to the world. God told me to make an ark so that I and my family might escape." The people made fun of him. Still Noah watered the cedars and they kept growing. The people asked again, "What are you doing?" Noah answered them in the same way as before. They still mocked him. Finally Noah cut down the trees. They asked again, "What are you doing?" Noah answered, "What I promised," and he continued to warn the people [of the flood]. When they still did not repent, God brought the flood.

(Midrash Tanhuma, Noah 5)

The rabbis found troubling the notion that God would so deeply regret the creation of human beings and that without warning destroy an entire generation. The many popular renditions of Noah's ark with all its friendly animals notwithstanding, this is not a child's story. It was deeply disconcerting for the rabbis to imagine a God who would completely wipe out a generation and save but one family. After all, God had disregarded the angels who argued against the creation of man and woman, casting Truth to the ground.

The rabbis recognized God's compassion as well as God's justice. They knew that human nature was often corrupt. They were keenly aware of their own shortcomings and transgressions. Thus they were certain that built into the world there must be a mechanism for repair, for correcting mistakes, for forgiving transgressions. Humanity could not otherwise be sustained. The world as they experienced it stood on a foundation of repentance. In fact, one midrash claimed that repentance was one of the six things that preceded the creation of the world, for without it creation would return to chaos.

The story of the flood seemed to contradict that theological cornerstone. The midrashic account of the flood story presupposed that the people of Noah's generation had plenty of time to recognize the error of their ways, to atone for and change their pattern of behavior. It took years for the cedar trees to grow and months to construct the ark. The people were given fair warning and the opportunity for repentance, but they refused.

Repentance is so powerful a tool for humanity that the rabbis even picture the Pharaoh who enslaved the people of Israel repenting of his evil deeds. Telescoping many centuries, the rabbis imagine Pharaoh becoming king of Nineveh. When Jonah comes to prophesy the city's overthrow, it is Pharaoh, now turned king of the Ninevites, who encourages the people to atone.

The rabbis are not only trying to make sense of the biblical narratives in ways consistent with their theology, they are also addressing the human condition as they experience it. They recognize the heavy burden of wrongdoing, the weight of transgression that they themselves and others bear. But if Cain and Pharaoh can change, then they can as well. If one who murdered and one who enslaved can repent and be forgiven, then they too may find forgiveness.

A PERSONAL REFLECTION

Let us make the human in our image . . . (Genesis 1:26). God created the world with words. God spoke and the world came to be. Created in God's image, humans were given the power of speech so that they too might create. But I imagine that just as the angels argued over the creation of man and woman, so they quarreled over God's decision to give the gift of language to humanity. Consider this modern midrash I have written:

God decided to give words to man and woman, the power of language. But the angels objected, saying, "People will not know what to do with words. Are not our words of praise the most beautiful? Why do you need to hear the words of man and woman?"

God said, "I want to hear how human beings will form words of praise. You live forever, but they live for only an allotted number of years. Their words will be different."

So God filled sacks with words and gave them to the angels. Then God sent the angels down to earth to spread the words. In one sack God put long, difficult words, and in another God put words that were hard to spell. Because of the difficult words, linguists created dictionaries. Because of words that were hard to spell, teachers created spelling lists. And when the angels had finished distributing all the words to man and woman, they sat down with God and listened. They wanted to hear what people would do with the words.

It took some time for people to get accustomed to using words. Slowly they let each word form in their mouths. Carefully they added one word to another to another until they made sentences.

At first the angels laughed at how man and woman mispronounced words, made run-on sentences, and fashioned new words that made no sense. But when man and woman began to twist and turn the words into lies, the angels stopped laughing. They listened to people rolling precious words in the wet earth until they were covered with mud and creating curses. They heard people mixing words with thorns and giving birth to gossip.

The angels could bear no more. They pleaded with God to take back the gift of language: "Look at the mess people have made with Your words."

At first God regretted giving language to man and woman. God was about to send angels down to earth to gather all the words and return them to the heavens, when God and the angels heard a new sound.

People stirred soft music into words and created lullabies. Some of them were filled with love and others with longing.

People began mixing words with dance, and poetry was born. Some poems overflowed with joy and others with sorrow.

People joined laughter to words and created humor. "God," said the angels, "some of these jokes we do not understand." But God said, "You must live on earth to comprehend what makes people laugh."

People wove yearning and hope into words and offered prayer. They embroidered words with imagination and told stories. The angels sat on the edge of their clouds and listened. God asked the angels if they wanted to go down to earth and gather all the words and return them to the heavens.

One angel said, "We must not take back words, because people use them in song." But another argued, "People use words to fashion lies. Words are meant to speak the truth." Still another angel pleaded on behalf of man and woman, "They use language to create poetry and form prayers." But another countered, "Man and woman employ words to make curses, and they abuse words to produce gossip."

All the angels thought about the lies, the curses, and the gossip that people had created with the gift of words. They remembered how they had once enjoyed the earth's silence, and they considered how now the earth was filled with noise and argument. They were about to go down and take back the words they had given man and woman when one angel protested, "If we take back the words, we will never know the end of the stories the people are telling."

And it was so. God showed compassion to man and woman and let them keep the gift of words, for the sake of story.

WHERE DO YOU SEE YOURSELF IN THE STORY?

With which angel do you identify the most?

When have you felt like the angels who argued against the creation of human beings, when like those who argued for their creation?

What argument do you have with God about humanity's creation?

What grace, what compassion, have you experienced in your life?

What Makes Us Angry?
Eavesdropping on the First Argument

As we have already examined, the anger that Cain feels when God does not accept his sacrifice erupts into violence and results in the very first act of murder. But it was not just Cain's anger or Abel's murder that interested the rabbis. They wanted to know why what happened once upon a time continues to happen all the time. They explored the question of what makes people so angry that they lose control and are driven to destroy what they love the most and, in the process, themselves.

The rabbis tell of a person who takes a sharp knife and slowly, carefully peels the skin away from an apple. But the person is distracted, and the knife slips and injures the other hand. The rabbis ask: What should the person do? Should the injured hand revenge itself out of anger for the hurt that was inflicted upon it? Should it grab the knife and plunge it into the hand that injured it? Obviously, that is ridiculous. One hand seeks to heal the other.

We do not always heed such advice when it comes to wounds of the human heart. The midrashim in the following pages invite us to consider what makes us angry and to ask ourselves—do we seek revenge or healing?

THE MIDRASH

Cain said to his brother Abel . . . and when they were in the field, Cain set upon his brother Abel and killed him. (Genesis 4:8)

About what did they quarrel? "Come," said they, "let us divide the world." One took the land and the other the movables. The former said, "The land you stand on is mine," while the latter retorted, "What you are wearing is mine." One said: "Strip"; the other retorted: "Fly [off the ground])." Out of the quarrel, *Cain rose up against his brother Abel.*

Rabbi Joshua of Siknin said in Rabbi Levi's name: Both took land and both took movables, so about what did they quarrel? One said, "The Temple must be built in my area," while the other claimed, "It must be built in mine." For it is written, *And it came to pass, when they were in the field:* now *field* refers to naught but the Temple as you read, *Zion* [i.e., the Temple] *shall be plowed as a field* (Micah 3:12). Out of this argument, *Cain rose up against his brother Abel.*

Judah ben Rabbi said: Their quarrel was about the first Eve. Said Rabbi Aibu: The first Eve had returned to dust. Then about what was their quarrel? Said Rabbi Huna: A female twin was

**born with Abel, and each claimed her. The
one claimed: "I will have her, because I am the
firstborn"; while the other maintained: "I must
have her, because she was born with me."**

(Genesis Rabbah 22:7)

The clear and simple meaning of the text is that Cain
and Abel argued, and Cain attacked his brother
and killed him. However, the rabbis are concerned
about what is missing in the narrative. What did Cain
say to his brother, Abel? Over what did they quarrel?
The rabbis attempt to fill in the blanks.

The midrashim differ as to the nature of the
argument itself. The first midrash suggests that the
quarrel is an economic one. Abel is the shepherd; he
takes those things that can be carried, moved from one
place to another. Cain is the farmer; he claims the land.
But their agreement to divide property goes sour, and
conflict ensues.

According to Rabbi Joshua, the argument is not
concerned with property; it is not about who owns
what (the classic conflict between shepherd and farmer).
Rather the dispute is about religion, in whose area God
will choose to build the Temple. In order to arrive at
this surprising conclusion, the midrash refers to a verse
from the prophet Micah that implies that the word *field*
can be understood as a reference to the Temple in

Jerusalem. It does not matter that the prophet Micah is writing generations later than Genesis, or that at the time of Cain and Abel there was no Temple. For the rabbis, there is no early or late in the Bible. Any text from any time can be used to elucidate another. So according to this rabbi, the two brothers are each claiming that the holy sanctuary will be built on his land.

Judah ben Rabbi construes the argument between Cain and Abel to be about neither property nor religion, but a woman. This interpretation takes some flight of rabbinic imagination. Where is there evidence in the biblical text for any woman but Eve? The rabbi may be referring to the verse in Genesis regarding the creation of woman: *This one* at last *is bone of my bone,* implying that before Eve another woman must have been created.

But Rabbi Huna imagines that Abel had a twin sister. He posits a simple reason for the fatal argument— jealousy over this woman.

These midrashim do more than illustrate the textual playfulness and imaginative creativity of the rabbis. They offer us insight into the world in which the rabbis lived and allow us a glimpse into the economic, religious, and sexual quarrels that plagued their times. In expanding the story of Cain and Abel, the rabbis not only fill in what is missing in the biblical text, they give the narrative new life and make it meaningful for another generation. They also invite us to read our story into the ancient text.

A PERSONAL REFLECTION

Stephen King, the famous science fiction writer, once commented that his mother taught him, "If something terrifies you, say it three times and you'll be okay." King said, "That's why I write; I write about what terrifies me."

I believe we keep retelling the story of Cain and Abel for the same reason—because it terrifies us. And we hope that if we tell it enough, we will be okay. But we are not okay. A story three thousand years old, a story of anger and violence, still rings true. Only now one murder has become millions.

The rabbis understood that Cain murdered more than just Abel, a lone individual. They explain that when Genesis says, "The voice of your brother's blood cries to me from the ground," the word for blood (*dam*) is written in the plural (*d'mei*). More than just Abel's blood calls out for justice. It is joined by the blood of all his future descendants (Genesis Rabbah 22:9). One person contains an entire world. Cain murdered possibility, the future, a whole world.

Another midrash (from Midrash Tanhuma) suggests that not only did Cain kill his brother, Abel, and all his possible descendants, but also his act of violence shattered the harmony and order of all creation. This text imagines that in the beginning when God created the world, God fashioned each tree so that it could yield many different kinds of fruit. Then Cain killed his brother Abel and the trees went into mourning. From then on each tree would yield but one kind of fruit. Only in the world to come will the trees return to their full fruitfulness.

Something changed with the first murder—not only the relationship between one human being and another, but also the relationship between humanity and the natural world. For if Cain could act as he did with his brother, how might he act in the natural world that was his home? And so the Bible tells us that the earth would no longer yield its abundance to Cain, the farmer, and he was banished from the soil that he had stained with his brother's blood.

In my own reading of the story of Cain and Abel, I had always seen Cain as an evil person. I could not possibly sympathize with him. I identified him with bullies, tyrants, and despots throughout history, never with anyone I knew intimately, and least of all with myself. But the rabbis who wrote midrashim, seeking to find the reasons for Cain's rage, gave him a more human face. They asked me to consider putting on Cain's shoes for a moment, to see my own anger in his. When I reluctantly tried on Cain's shoes, I found that they fit a bit too comfortably.

Wearing those shoes, I felt Cain's resentment and outrage at life's unfairness. His brother was the favored one, and yet Cain also worked hard. For no apparent reason, Abel's offering was accepted and Cain's was not. It appeared as if even God had rejected him, as if God liked the shepherd, Abel, better than the farmer, Cain. I did not approve of Cain's response to rejection, but I could understand it.

When I teach this story to children today, I ask them to tell me if they ever feel angry like Cain. They do. I especially remember one child who drew a picture of a time when he felt like Cain. On a white piece of paper he had drawn two adults who were obviously yelling at one another. A small child was standing between them. When I asked the young boy to tell me about his drawing, he explained that the two adults were his parents. "And who is the person in the middle?" I asked. He was silent for a moment, and then he responded, "I am."

I asked him what he might like to tell his parents. He said, "I would like to tell them to stop." Then I wondered if he would show this picture to his parents and tell them what he had just told me. He didn't think he could.

There is much speculation in the midrashim about the nature of the argument between Cain and Abel.

The rabbis go to great lengths to fill in the words that the two brothers spoke to each other. But after listening to this little boy who held the anger of Cain inside, I thought that perhaps there were no missing words. The content of the quarrel between Cain and Abel does not really matter all that much. What matters are our own quarrels and how we choose to resolve them, what we do with our own justifiable rage when life is unfair.

I sometimes think that God wanted to say the same words as that little boy, to tell the two brothers to stop. But God couldn't, for God had given freedom to Cain and Abel. I sometimes think that Cain wanted to speak as well, to say "Stop!"—but did not know how. Perhaps because Cain couldn't tell Abel to stop taunting him with his good fortune, or because he couldn't tell God to help stop the pain he was feeling, he exploded; he killed his brother. There were no missing words, and that was the problem.

Another midrash teaches that when iron was created, the trees began to tremble.

THE MIDRASH

Iron spoke to them, "Why do you tremble? Let none of your wood enter me, and not one of you will be harmed."

(Genesis Rabbah 5:9)

When wood and iron are joined, they form an ax. The ax can destroy the tree from which it was created, but only with the tree's cooperation. We too can be our own worst enemy or our own best friend.

WHERE DO YOU SEE YOURSELF IN THE STORY?

Read the whole story of Cain and Abel in Genesis 4. Then, considering the following questions, create your own midrash on the Cain and Abel story.

In your family, community, state, and/or nation, what divisions generate the most controversy and frequently lead to violent encounters?

What might a dialogue between Cain and Abel have sounded like?

Consider the possibility that the brothers were unable to express their anger and that what was most important was left unspoken. What are some of the missing words that you need to speak?

Who Is Responsible?
Blaming God for our Shortcomings

I n the face of evil, confronted by senseless tragedy, no matter how deep our faith, we cannot help questioning God. Theological rationalizations do not comfort us at the raw edges of life. We have all heard the explanations of those who seek to carve meaning out of the emptiness: God must have a reason that we cannot fathom. Whatever happens is meant to be. Only the tough are tested; we are not given more than we can bear. Pain makes us stronger, more sensitive to others. If we are honest with ourselves, however, none of these explanations rings true. We want to respond: what kind of God is this?

The rabbis are not afraid to pose the questions that we often are reluctant to ask for fear they might be considered blasphemous. For the rabbis, faith is about the mind as well as the soul. Their theology may not be ours, but their willingness to ask the hard questions, to voice their deepest doubts, gives us permission to do the same.

For the next few pages, suspend your theological assumptions; listen to the different arguments of the rabbis and see which most closely reflects your own.

The Lord said to Cain, "Where is Abel, your brother?" And he said, "I do not know. Am I my brother's keeper?" Then God said, "What have you done? Hark, your brother's blood cries out to Me from the ground." (Genesis 4:9–10)

Rabbi Shimon bar Yohai said, This is a difficult thing to say and it is impossible to say it clearly. Once two athletes were wrestling before the king. If the king wished, they could be separated, but he did not want them separated. One overcame the other and killed him. The loser cried out as he died: "Who will get justice for me from the king?" Thus: *The voice of your brother's blood cries to Me from the ground.*

(Genesis Rabbah 22:9)

It is clear from the opening line that Rabbi Shimon bar Yohai is speaking about a subject that deeply disturbs him. As a religious person, he is reluctant to challenge traditional theology, hesitant to question the accepted understanding of the Genesis passage about Cain. The plain understanding of the biblical text is that Cain has killed his brother. Despite Cain's attempts to avoid blame for Abel's death, God calls Cain to account. Cain is at fault; he murdered Abel and must be punished.

But Rabbi Shimon bar Yohai begins to wonder whether God could have arranged things differently. The two athletes in the midrash represent Cain and Abel. The king is God. Cain and Abel are fighting in full view of God. God knows very well what is going to happen, and if God wishes, God has the power to separate the two brothers, stop the fight, and prevent the murder. Yet God does nothing. The loser of the fight, Abel, cries out as he dies, accusing God, not Cain, of murder.

Assuredly, the rabbi is concerned not only with Abel's death at the hands of Cain, but with the deaths and tragedies in his own time. His question, filled with the pain and sorrow of his own generation (when so many Jews were dying at the hands of the Roman Empire), is difficult to ask, but he asks it nonetheless: where is God?

Another midrash offers a different understanding of this same text.

THE MIDRASH

As soon as the Holy One, the blessed One said to Cain: *"Where is Abel, your brother?"* Cain replied: *"I do not know. Am I my brother's keeper? You are the keeper of all creatures; yet, you ask me?"* To what may this be compared? To a thief who stole vessels by night and was not caught. In the morning, the guard caught him and asked: "Why did you steal the vessels?" To which the thief replied: "I stole them, but I did not neglect my job. But your job is to guard the gate, why did you neglect your job?" . . . So too Cain said: "I did kill Abel because You created in me the evil inclination. You are the guard of all; yet You allowed me to kill him. You are the one who killed him. Had you accepted my sacrifice the same as his, I would not have been jealous of him." Immediately, God answered: "What have *you* done? The *voice of your brother's blood calls out. . . .*"

(Midrash Tanhuma, Bereshit 9)

This midrash compares Cain to a thief who steals and God to the guard who does not stop the theft. The thief is simply living up to the person he is. His task is stealing. It is the guard, who does not stop the thief, who is remiss in his duty and is therefore responsible for the stolen goods. As the thief accepts no blame, so Cain relinquishes accountability. After all, Cain argues, God created within him the inclination to do evil. God chose not to stop the murder. Furthermore, because God did not accept his sacrifice, God caused the jealousy that lead to his killing Abel. The midrash accepts none of these excuses. Neither life's unfairness nor human nature can be offered as extenuating circumstances. Cain cannot claim to be the victim, driven by biological forces or life situations beyond his control. God dismisses all Cain's arguments without discussion and places responsibility directly upon him.[7]

The author reads into Cain's attempt to avoid accountability the excuses of his own generation. Yet perhaps at the same time, he also considers the validity of Cain's arguments. After all, he cannot help wondering with Rabbi Shimon bar Yohai about God's lack of intervention in the course of human tragedy. Still, despite doubts, he answers Rabbi Shimon by clearly exonerating God and underscoring human responsibility.

The question "Where is God?" continues to be asked in the face of major disasters brought about by natural causes (hurricanes, earthquakes) or by human actions (Holocaust, genocide). The rabbis do not avoid challenging established conceptions of God, asking the hard questions others might consider blasphemous. They open a theological conversation and invite us to continue that dialogue in our own day.

A PERSONAL REFLECTION

We yearn to see meaning behind all that happens in life. We want order, an explanation, even if we cannot discern it. When we face illness, we say it must be for some reason, perhaps to teach us gratitude or empathy, perhaps to make us stronger. Someone dies, and we often say that it was meant to be, that it must have been God's will. Tragedies on major scales abound— famine, disease, and genocide—and we search for God's presence in them. When we can't readily detect it, we assume it is a deficiency on our part. We say that in God's mysterious plan, some things are simply beyond human understanding. And people think that such statements are expressions of faith.

This is a difficult thing to say, and perhaps it is impossible to say it clearly. But I think such statements are blasphemy. Why would God bring disease to make people stronger? Why would God cause children to die of starvation and people to perish in a hurricane? Why would God permit one person to murder another and governments to wipe out an entire people? Why would God design a world where such things—and worse— can happen? This is not the God I believe in.

Following Hurricane Katrina a church posted a sign that read, "God gives us the storm to show us that He is the only shelter." This is not an image of a faithful and loving God, but of an abusive, capricious parent enthroned on high.

We often say that things are meant to be. I have said those words myself. But I don't really believe them. Nothing happens the way it does because it was somehow designed at some time before we counted time, because some cosmic superpower so decreed it. Some things happen because of human neglect, greed, and hate. And some things happen by the chaos wrought by nature, by chance without any reason. They aren't meant to be. They just are.

Religion tells us what to do with the realities we face. God gives us the strength to change those things that can and must be changed. And God helps us to confront those things that happen unfairly, for no good reason. God helps us deal with what is beyond our control, what can't be changed.

I used to think that we are where we are for a preordained reason. But I no longer believe that is true. We are where we are, and it is up to us whether there is a purpose in it or not. Places, circumstances, and encounters aren't inherently meaningful; we make them meaningful, we give them purpose.

Sinai without the Ten Commandments is just another mountain. Matzah (unleavened bread) without the story of the Exodus is just a tasteless cracker. Wine without a blessing is just another alcoholic beverage. Friday night without candles, challah, and kiddush is just the end of the week. December 25 without the story of Christmas is just another winter day. We make Shabbat. We sanctify moments. We confer significance on time. We let God into our lives, or we keep God out.

On the one hand, we stand with Rabbi Shimon bar Yohai, shaking our fist at God. It is not just the blood of Abel but the blood of many generations that cries out. We are outraged at the world unredeemed, torn by war, pained by natural disasters, and devastated by human failings, demanding an answer to the perennial question: where are You?

On the other hand, we recognize our human responsibility to make a world that is kinder and more just, where we *are* our brother's keeper. Human beings may ask, "Where is God?" But in the Garden of Eden, it is God who asks the more important question to Adam and so to each of us: "Where are you?"

WHERE DO YOU SEE YOURSELF IN THE STORY?

What is difficult for you to say about your faith, about God?

What question do you have of God, and what question does God have of you?

Give a voice to Abel's blood that calls out to God.

The first question in the Bible is addressed to Adam in the Garden of Eden after he has eaten of the fruit from the tree of knowledge of good and evil: "Where are you?" Then God asks Cain after he has murdered Abel: "Where is your brother?" How would you answer those two questions?

What if the Angels Should Come Too Late?
Getting On With It, When you Can't Get Over It

One of the most difficult stories in the Bible is the binding of Isaac. What kind of God would ask a father to take his beloved son up a mountain to sacrifice him? What kind of God would wait until the very last moment to intervene, restrain the father's hand, and release the son, Isaac, who was trembling beneath the knife? The rabbis turn the story's focus from God to Isaac. They identify with Isaac because his experience most resembles their own. They wonder aloud about those many Isaacs who did not survive and about how those who escaped the knife could go on.

Abraham Joshua Heschel, the renowned twentieth-century philosopher and rabbi, remembered being taught the story of Isaac's binding when he was a child. Upon hearing the angel tell Abraham not to lay a hand upon Isaac, Heschel began to weep. Despite his teacher's reassurance that Isaac was saved, the young Heschel was not consoled. He asked, "But rabbi, supposing the angel had come a second too late?" The rabbi explained that an angel can never come late. But Heschel concluded,

"An angel cannot be late, but man, made of flesh and blood, may be."[8]

In the following midrashim, the rabbis address us at our most vulnerable, when we fear that no one will come to rescue us. They ask us to imagine how we can face our greatest fears and not be defeated by them.

THE MIDRASH

Abraham took the wood for the burnt offering and put it on his son Isaac. He himself took the firestone and the knife; and the two walked off together. (Genesis 22:6)

Abraham then returned to his servants, and they departed together for Beersheva; and Abraham stayed in Beersheva. (Genesis 22:19)

And Isaac, where was he? Rabbi Berekiah said: . . . He sent him to Shem to study Torah, and there he remained for three years. And Isaac, where was he? Rabbi Yose ben Haninah replied: He sent him home in the night, for fear of the Evil Eye.

(Genesis Rabbah 56:11)

And Isaac, where was he? The Holy One, the blessed One, brought him into the Garden of Eden, and there he stayed three years.

(Midrash Hagadol on Genesis 22:19)[9]

And Isaac, where was he? The angels bore him to Paradise, where he tarried three years, to be healed from the wound inflicted upon him by Abraham on the occasion of the *Akedah* [the binding of Isaac].

(Abarbanel on Genesis 22:19)[10]

Abraham and Isaac walked up Mount Moriah together. But at the conclusion of the traumatic encounter on the mountain, Abraham returned to Beersheba with only his servants. Isaac was not with him. Where was Isaac? For three years Isaac is absent from the biblical narrative, until he marries Rebecca. The rabbis question what happened to Isaac during that time, and they offer different responses.

Something extraordinary happened on the mountain. Abraham tied his son to the altar and stood above him with a knife in his hand. One midrash imagines that as Abraham stretched forth his hand, he wept, and his tears fell into Isaac's eyes. Isaac was saved at the last moment, but the shock of the ordeal had to have altered him and his understanding of the world. What if the angel had come too late? How could Isaac have once again taken his father's hand, which had held the sacrificial knife, as he had done on the journey up the mountain? How could he continue to trust his father, or anyone else? Where could he find the faith to go on?

Because we do not encounter Isaac again until he marries Rebecca, all the midrashim assume that it took him three years to repair the damage to his soul. For Rabbi Berekiah, study of Torah was the answer to Isaac's despair. Of course at the time of the Genesis narrative there was as yet no Torah, but the midrash has no problem telescoping the years and reading back into the text a later time when Torah study was seen as an antidote to many ills. Rabbi Berekiah sees in the study of Torah a way of countering the desolation of his own generation. Just as Isaac faced imminent danger, so did the Jews living in the rabbi's time. If Torah study could enable Isaac to continue, then surely Torah was an antidote to the hopelessness of his own days.

Rabbi Yose ben Haninah suggests that Abraham sent Isaac home under cover of dark before he returned with his servants. Abraham feared that people would look upon Isaac differently because of his narrow escape from death. Perhaps he believed that Isaac's last-minute reprieve would make him vulnerable to misfortune. According to popular superstition, publicizing good luck might only tempt the forces of evil.

The first selections, which address the question of what happened to Isaac, are from Genesis Rabbah, a collection of midrashim on the book of Genesis edited in the fifth and sixth centuries. The third text, which suggests that Isaac spent three years in the Garden of

Eden or Paradise, is from Midrash Hagadol, a thirteenth-century rabbinic collection of midrashim. Isaac Abrabanel, who provides the striking statement that Isaac was actually wounded by his father, was a well-known statesman, philosopher, and biblical commentator. He wrote during the fifteenth century, at the time of the Jewish expulsion from Spain.

Both Midrash Hagadol and Abrabanel reflect the history of their own period. Having experienced the nightmare of the Crusades (during which Christians slaughtered thousands of Jews en route to their confrontations with Muslims in the Holy Land) and later the devastation caused by the Inquisition and the expulsion of the Jews from Spain and Portugal, the writers see their people's persecutions mirrored in the binding of Isaac. As Isaac was bound to the altar ready to be sacrificed, so they were bound by outside forces and were prepared, like their ancestor the patriarch Isaac, to sacrifice their lives for their faith.

But for Jews in the Middle Ages, something was different. They often were not saved from death. No one intervened at the last moment to withhold the knife. The angel did come too late. There were thousands of Isaacs in those centuries, but they were all sacrificed.

A contemporary poem written by Hillel Bavli tells the story of a group of young Jewish women in Warsaw who, about to be raped by Nazi soldiers, chose martyrdom over defilement. They saw themselves as modern Isaacs.

Abraham responded to God's command to sacrifice Isaac by saying, "Here I am." So the poet imagines the women praying to the matriarch, Sarah: "Here we are. We have met the test of Isaac's binding."

The Bible clearly tells us that Abraham did not raise his hand against Isaac (Genesis 22:12), but the experience of the Jewish people reflects a different outcome. That may be why Abrabanel states that Isaac was mortally wounded and taken to Paradise, where the angels healed him. Perhaps those words reflect not only the dark reality of the age in which they were written, but also the hope and the promise that all the Jewish martyrs will be healed and that, like Isaac, the people of Israel will survive.

A PERSONAL REFLECTION

The reading prescribed for the Jewish New Year, Rosh Hashanah, is Genesis 22, the story of Abraham and Isaac. Every year it's the same story. In Hebrew, we call it the *Akedah*, which means binding. Abraham walks Isaac up the mountain and prepares to sacrifice him, believing he is obeying God's command. Only at the last moment is Isaac saved and a ram sacrificed in his place. Every year the same story, but each year it somehow acquires a different meaning as we hear it anew, refracted through the lens of our personal experiences.

So often we focus on Abraham. What was he thinking when he heard what he believed was God's call to sacrifice his beloved son? Why didn't he challenge God as he did when God announced that Sodom and Gomorrah would be destroyed? Why didn't he talk to Sarah or even to Isaac about what he planned to do?

Sometimes we do not feel all that in control of our world. We do not identify with Abraham, so full of trust, so certain that he knows just what to do. We feel more like Isaac—vulnerable and apprehensive, propelled by forces beyond our control, going about our daily tasks filled with doubts, living with a knife hanging over our heads, never knowing if there will be a reprieve. At times we are all Isaac, uncertain of the future and afraid.

I often wonder how Isaac managed to get up after being tied down. How did he succeed in living when he had come so close to death, when all that he believed had been altered? He was able to walk up the mountain because he had faith. He went with his father in whom he had trusted, confident that his people would be as many as the grains of sand and the lights of the stars. But he walked down the mountain alone. Going up the mountain, he held his father's hand. What did he hold coming down? In what and in whom could he still believe?

The first thing Isaac learned was that his mother, Sarah, had died. Surely his faith in a benevolent universe was shaken; he could never again be fully comforted by promises, divine or otherwise. On their journey up the mountain, Abraham had told Isaac that everything would be all right. No one would ever be able to tell him that again. The rabbis refer to Isaac's God as *Pachad Yitzchak*, the Fear of Isaac.

After the traumatic encounter on the mountain, the rabbis ask, "And Isaac, where was he?" They answer, "The Holy One brought him into the Garden of Eden and there he stayed three years." What was he doing all that time in Paradise? The midrash tells us, "The angels were healing him."

So many times when we confront difficulties, when we are hurt or face loss, people tell us we will get over it, everything will be okay. But I don't imagine Isaac ever got over it; rather, the angels taught him how to heal, how to get on with it.

The name of Isaac's God means "fear," but Isaac's name means "laughter." I don't think he was given this name only because Abraham and Sarah laughed when they heard that they would have a son in their old age. I think that Isaac laughed too. The angels taught him to laugh in the face of the unknown and wrestle joy out of despair.

How do we get on with it when we can't get over it, find hope and wrestle joy when like Isaac we face fear, loss, and uncertainty? The first thing we learn about Isaac after the mountain is that he meets and marries Rebecca. He is able to get on with it because he finds someone with whom to go on, someone to share his anguish, someone who listens and brings comfort. Like Isaac, we all need someone who will give us a hand when necessary and a push when required. Loneliness is the perfect breeding ground for despair. Sometimes when we are going through a hard time, when we are staring at a knife poised just above us, what is most important is someone else's hand.

I believe the second thing the angels taught Isaac was to forget some things and forgive others. We easily forget appointments, but we remember grudges for years. We misplace things but never resentments. And those grudges and resentments eat away at our spirit and corrode our souls.

If every day Isaac woke up and relived the day on the mountain when his father almost sacrificed him, I don't think he would have ever gotten out of bed. The experience of being bound to an altar changed Isaac. He could never return to the innocence he had once known. He would never be the person who with light-hearted step climbed the mountain. But even though he could not wipe the experience from his memory, he could forgive his father and his God, look at Rebecca and his children, and focus on the present moment. And he could still find reason for laughter.

Sometimes we are so stuck in a past that we cannot change, or so afraid of a future over which we have limited control, that we don't really appreciate the present—the very moment before us. We worry about what happened or what will happen, and we forget about what is happening. I have been there; we all have. We squander the one thing we have for certain—now.

Finally, the last thing that the angels gave Isaac was hope. When we face trauma, when everything we believe in is turned upside down, hope is all there is to keep us from giving up or giving in. It is what enables us to get up and walk down the mountain, to keep planting trees even if we may not be around to see them grow and offer shade.

When times have been especially difficult in my life, I would look at the evening sky to find the first star, and then I would repeat in my heart a rhyme remembered from my childhood:

Star light, star bright,
First star I see tonight,
I wish I may, I wish I might
Have the wish I wish tonight.

Despite the persistence of this childhood fantasy, I know that there is a difference between wishing and hoping. Wishing leaves the work up to someone else; it is passive; it asks nothing of us. Hoping demands that we make a commitment to work toward whatever it is we hope for. Whenever I confront my personal trials and fears, I try to heed the wisdom of Isaac's healing angels. Find support in another. Forget some things and forgive others. Laugh whenever possible and celebrate whenever you can. Embrace the present moment. And never, never give up hope.

WHERE DO YOU SEE YOURSELF IN THE STORY?

Are there times you have felt like Isaac, bound to a situation with little promise of release?

How do you get on with it, when you can't get over it?

Who or what is your saving angel?

God Is in This Place, but I Did Not Know It
Finding Holiness in Unexpected Places

e expect revelation to come from mountaintops. Amidst the audiovisual fireworks of Sinai, it is hard to miss the divine. But the rabbis wonder about less-than-spectacular landscapes, ordinary moments, events of everyday life. When the sacred doesn't shout, how do we notice it?

I once visited the rain forest in Costa Rica. During our forest tour, the guide introduced us to a variety of birds, butterflies, and plants. At one point, he stopped to point out an exotic bird, the quetzal. "I can't see it!" I exclaimed. He extended a hand to direct my vision and said in a whisper, "Look right over there."

I still couldn't see it. I was growing irritated and frustrated, since it seemed that everyone around me *did* see it and were saying things like, "Wow! Incredible!"

The guide placed a gentle hand on my shoulder. "Stay very quiet, don't move, be patient, and keep looking straight ahead." I finally did as directed and then I saw it—an extraordinarily beautiful bird with iridescent colors hidden among the dense growth of the trees.

The midrashim in the next chapter remind us to stop long enough to realize that the ground we stand on is holy, to notice a landscape touched by God's creative hand and kept sacred by human effort. They ask us to think about what we miss when we are too hurried to pay attention.

THE MIDRASH

On the third day Abraham looked up and saw the place from afar. Then Abraham said to his servants, "You stay here with the donkey. The boy [Isaac] and I will go up there; we will worship and we will return to you." (Genesis 22:4–5)

And saw the place from afar. What did Abraham see? He saw a cloud enveloping the mountain and said: "It appears that this is the place where the Holy One . . . told me to sacrifice my son." Abraham then said to Isaac: "My son, do you see what I see?" "Yes," Isaac replied. Abraham then asked his companions: "Do you see what I see?" "No," they answered. Abraham said, "Since you do not see it, *you stay here with the donkey* [*im hahamor*] because you are like the donkey [*am hahamor*]: it can't see anything either."

(Genesis Rabbah 56:1–2)

This Genesis text is part of the longer narrative of the binding of Isaac. Abraham, Isaac, and two servants begin the journey without knowing their precise destination. On the third day of their travels, Abraham becomes aware that the mountain where they have arrived is, in fact, the place where God wants him to take Isaac.

The midrash is concerned with two matters. First, since God has not told him specifically, how does Abraham know which is the place to which God has intended for him to take Isaac? It could be one of many mountains. After all, there are no more messages from God telling Abraham he has arrived at his destination, nor are there road signs announcing: "Stop, this is a holy mountain."

The midrash fills in the blanks. Abraham sees something different on this mountain: a cloud envelops it. To Abraham this is a sign marking this place as holy, the location where God intends Abraham to take his son.

But what about the companions? Abraham has not told them of God's command to sacrifice his son. They think they are simply accompanying Abraham and Isaac as they sacrifice an animal in gratitude to God.

In fact, Abraham tells no one what he believes God has asked him to do. He rises early in the morning, presumably before his wife, Sarah, awakens, so as to avoid her questions about where he and Isaac are going. Certainly she would have stopped Abraham from embarking on this terrifying journey with the son of their old age.

Strikingly, Abraham also declines to talk to God or challenge God's command as he had done when God told him about the impending destruction of Sodom and Gomorrah. In the biblical text, he says nothing to Isaac either.

How did Abraham and Isaac recognize what their companions did not? Abraham, Isaac, and the companions all stand in the same place, but they see different things. Abraham and Isaac are attuned to the holy; their eyes are open to the sacred. The companions' eyes are closed; they see only the commonplace.

In a play on words, the midrash suggests that the companions are to stay with the donkey [im hahamor] because they are donkey-like people [am hahamor]. Their vision is no different from the animals'.

The midrash is not just about what happened in Genesis; it is about what was happening in the lives of the generation of the rabbis who wrote this narrative. Overburdened by demands of everyday life, outside pressures, and fears, the people focused primarily on survival. There were no doubt trials and ordeals when God seemed absent. The rabbis sought to help them see beyond the daily grind, the drudgery of routine; to find the transcendence in the commonplace.

The midrash addresses us as well. We are asked to wonder whether we are more like the companions or like Abraham. Do we pass by places and ignore their significance? Do we move from moment to moment, easily distracted, never fully present? And if we live that way, what do we miss?

Another midrash, reflecting on God's choice of a thorn bush to reveal the divine presence to Moses, reminds us to look for the extraordinary in the ordinary.

The book of Exodus describes the moment when God is revealed to Moses:

Now Moses, tending the flock of his father-in-law Jethro, the priest of Midian, drove the flock into the wilderness, and came to Horeb, the mountain of God. An angel of the Lord appeared to him in a blazing fire out of a thorn bush. He gazed, and there was a bush all aflame, yet the bush was not consumed. Moses said, "I must turn aside to look at this marvelous sight; why doesn't the thorn bush burn up?" When the Lord saw that he had turned aside to see, God called to him out of the bush: "Moses! Moses!" He answered, "Here I am." And God said, "Do not come closer. Remove your sandals from your feet, for the place on which you stand is holy." (Exodus 3:1–5)

The rabbis assume that there is nothing insignificant in the Torah. It cannot be just by chance that God chooses to speak to Moses out of a thorn bush.

Remember, each word, even every letter, is there for a purpose. Therefore, they wonder, why the choice of this particular plant instead of another?

The rabbis offer numerous suggestions about why God chose the thorn bush to call Moses to the task of freeing his people from Egyptian bondage. The bush becomes a symbol of Israel's suffering and of God's promise that just as fire does not consume the bush, so Egypt will not destroy Israel (Exodus Rabbah 2:25).

One rabbi suggests another reason for the unusual choice. Commenting on the verse, *An angel of the Lord appeared to him* [Moses] *in a blazing fire out of a thorn bush* (Exodus 3:2), he offers the following interpretation:

THE MIDRASH

A certain heathen asked Rabbi Joshua ben Karhah: "Why did the Holy One, the blessed One, speak to Moses out of a thorn bush?" He said to him: "Had it been out of a carob, or out of a sycamore, you would ask the same question. But I cannot send you away empty-handed. Why then out of a thorn bush? To teach you that there is no space free of the divine presence, not even a thorn bush."

(Exodus Rabbah 2:9)

The heathen does not fool Rabbi Joshua. The rabbi realizes that his questioner is a skeptic and would query the text no matter what it said. Yet the rabbi does not dismiss the inquiry as mere mockery, but recognizes that the question provides an important teaching moment. God does not choose a fruit tree or a shade tree as the place of revelation, but a small bush, one with thorns, precisely because it is likely to be passed over, avoided. God's presence is everywhere, even in the places where we are least likely to look. There are no signposts along the way that say, watch for holy spots, or slow down for divine revelation, or be prepared to stop for sacred presence.

We often don't notice the sacred because we, unlike Moses, don't turn aside to see. Moses didn't go out seeking revelation. He was simply going about his everyday business of tending sheep. It was not that unusual in the desert for a bush to be aflame; what was striking was the fact that it was not consumed. Others might have passed by and never even noticed, because they did not pause long enough to recognize the holy in the midst of the mundane. Rabbi Joshua reminds the reader that if God can appear to Moses in something as seemingly insignificant as a thorn bush, God can be present to us at all times and in all places. We just need to stop and pay attention.

Moments of revelation abound, but either from inattention or from fear we miss the opportunity to see. When Jacob flees the wrath of his brother, Esau, he spends the night alone. He dreams of a ladder that reaches up to the sky with angels of God going up and down it. When he awakes from his dream, he realizes that God was present in that place, but he did not know it.

THE MIDRASH

Jacob left Beersheva and set out for Haran. He came upon a certain place and stopped there for the night, for the sun had set. Taking one of the stones of that place, he put it under his head and lay down in that place. He had a dream; a ladder was set on the ground and its top reached to the sky, and angels of God were ascending and descending. (Genesis 28:10–12)

The midrash wonders who the angels are intended to represent and why they first ascend and then descend. After all, wouldn't it make more sense for angels first to come down to earth and then to ascend again to the heavens? One midrash suggests the angels represent the different nations that will enslave Israel. They ascend in power but they are ultimately defeated (descend).

Therefore fear not, Jacob, my servant. (Jeremiah 30:10)

This speaks of Jacob, of whom it is written, *and he dreamed, and behold, a ladder set up on the earth . . . and behold the angels of God ascending and descending on it.*

Rabbi Berekiah and Rabbi Helbo and Rabbi Shimon bar Yohai in the name of Rabbi Meir said: It teaches that the Holy One, the blessed One, showed Jacob the Prince[s] of Babylon . . . of Media [Persia] . . . of Greece . . . and of Edom [Rome] ascending and descending. Then God said to Jacob: "You also ascend." Our father Jacob was afraid, and thought: Perhaps, heaven forbid, in the same way as these nations descended, I will also have to descend. Said the Holy One, the blessed One: *Fear not, Jacob my servant.* **Once you ascend there will be no descent for you. Jacob would not believe and did not ascend.**

(Leviticus Rabbah 29:2 and Pesikta De-Rab Kahana 23:2)

In the midrash Jacob asks if because of his lack of faith or his unwillingness to ascend Israel will always be under foreign domination. The midrash concludes with the following biblical promise:

Do not be dismayed, O Israel; for I will save you from afar . . . and your seed from the land of their captivity. . . . (Jeremiah 30:10)

The rabbis are reading subsequent foreign rulers over Israel back into the biblical text. On the one hand, they seek to explain the real historical circumstances of Israel's oppression, and on the other, they give Israel reason to hope for a future redemption. Even though Israel has suffered under many kingdoms, the midrash offers the people an antidote to despair.

While making sense of national events, the midrash also addresses the individual. Unlike Moses, Jacob is afraid. Moses turns aside to see God's presence; Jacob turns away. To live in the presence of God requires not only attentiveness but also courage. Faith is not for the weak at heart; it often demands leaping over an abyss without ever knowing if you are going to land on solid ground. Afraid of taking such a risk, of possible failure, blinded by fear and doubt, Jacob fails to see his opportunity to change the course of history. In the midrash, God tells Jacob what he missed by not ascending, by fearing that he might fall. Now the moment has passed; it is too late. Like Jacob, we too miss opportunities to change the course of our lives. And once the moment has passed, it is not likely to present itself again soon.

A Jewish story tells about a young boy who had read many stories about the prophet Elijah. He believed that if he could meet the prophet, his whole life would change. His father told him that if he stayed awake all night studying, perhaps Elijah would come to greet him.

The boy did as his father instructed. In the middle of the night, there was a knock on the door. But when the boy opened it, all he saw was a lonely old beggar who wanted to talk and to eat. The boy dismissed the elderly man, saying he had no time for such an intrusion.

The next day the boy's father asked his son whether Elijah had come to visit him during the night. The boy responded that only an old beggar had come to interrupt his studies, and he had sent him away. The father told his son that the old beggar was in fact Elijah the prophet, and that he had missed the opportunity of speaking with him. From that day on, the boy always greeted and welcomed people, no matter how busy he was. He is still waiting for Elijah.

A PERSONAL REFLECTION

One summer I spent many long hours in airports. I considered airline terminals to be necessary gateways to get me where I wanted to go, nothing more. What was supposed to happen was what would occur in the place where I was going.

That summer I discovered that what is supposed to happen may occur wherever you are, and that the corridors leading to your destinations may in fact be more significant than the destinations themselves.

I had just visited my family in Philadelphia. I arrived at the airport ready to return home to Indianapolis. The flight was delayed, and so I bought some frozen yogurt and sat down to read a book. In an hour, we boarded the plane. But as often happens, three hours later, close to midnight, we were still on the runway. And the book wasn't that good. The cabin was hot, and I was thirsty.

I am not supposed to be here, I grumbled to myself. I have appointments tomorrow and work waiting on my desk. My husband had planned to pick me up at the airport. We were going out to dinner. I am not supposed to be here.

Finally the flight was canceled. After waiting an hour in line to rebook a flight for the next morning, I found my way to a small hotel near the airport. It was two in the morning. It would be a very short night.

I woke up early and returned to the airport, finally boarding my flight home. I found myself seated next to a gentleman from Indianapolis. He too had been booked on the canceled flight the night before. We commiserated. Neither of us was supposed to be there.

He told me a bit about himself. And though I seldom disclose to a stranger on an airplane that I am a rabbi, something prompted me to do so. "For years," my seat companion began, "I have had questions I wanted to ask a rabbi. . . ." Frustration and exhaustion gave way to dialogue and encounter. I had been worrying about what the canceled flight had caused me to miss, not about what it would allow me to find.

Every place contains holy sparks; we just have to turn aside to see them for what they are. No things, not even thorn bushes, are useless unless we treat them as useless. No moments, whether we are tending sheep like Moses or traveling on an airplane, are meaningless unless we squander them. No places, whether Mount Moriah or an airport terminal, are insignificant unless we overlook them.

In our rush to get where we are going, to do what we think we should be doing, we miss countless moments of revelation because we do not pay attention. We can choose to stay with the donkey, unaware of God's presence—or we can ascend the ladder with the angels and see the divine even in the ground beneath our feet.

WHERE DO YOU SEE YOURSELF IN THE STORY?

Are there times when you are more like the companions and other times when you are more like Abraham in the first midrash?

Have you ever felt like Jacob, afraid to ascend the ladder for fear of falling?

When have you felt you were standing on holy ground?

What keeps you from turning aside to see, from ascending the ladder?

Who Is the First to Cross the Sea?
Taking Risks for Freedom

For most of us the miracle of the Exodus is the improbable scenario in which a sea splits apart at just the right moment, allowing a group of slaves to walk on dry land and to escape their taskmasters. This spectacle seems to have been made for film.

Some people understand this narrative as a powerful example of miraculous intervention in natural law. Others, more skeptical, try to reconcile possible natural occurrences with the extraordinary event, suggesting that a strong tide or wind might have accounted for the phenomenon of the dividing waters.

The supernatural explanation for the Exodus creates a clear disconnect between science and religion. The naturalist understanding sees nothing more than a favorable weather report. Neither approach gets to the heart of the story.

In the midrashim in the following pages, the rabbis focus neither on meteorology nor on theology. They wonder instead: what would allow a generation of slaves, who had learned subservience and dependence, to risk safety for freedom? They focus on change—not an unprecedented one in or beyond the natural order, but an unanticipated one in the human order. The rabbis are not writing only about the generation of the Exodus; they are addressing their own generation and ours. They understand the biblical name for Egypt, *Mitzraim*, to be related to the Hebrew word for narrows, *metzar*. They base this on a phrase from Psalm 118: *Out of the narrows* [metzar] *I called to God*. When the rabbis refer to Egypt, they are also talking about the narrow places where we get stuck, as our ancestors got stuck in Egypt.

THE MIDRASH

But they were rebellious at the sea, at the Red Sea. (Psalms 106:7)

Why does the verse repeat "at the sea"? Because the people rebelled first at the sea when they refused to cross. It was only the tribe of Judah who induced them to cross by plunging in first and sanctifying the name of the Holy One, the blessed One, as it is stated (Psalm 114:1): *When Israel came from out of Egypt . . . Judah became his sanctuary.* And how do we know that the people rebelled a second time at the Red Sea? When they had plunged into the sea bed, they found it was full of clay, because it was still wet from

the water, and so it formed a kind of clay, as it is stated (Habakkuk 3:15): *You have trodden the sea with Your horses, through the clay of mighty water.* On that occasion the tribe of Reuben said to Simeon: In Egypt we had clay, and now, in the sea, once again we have clay. In Egypt we had mortar and bricks, and now, in the sea, once again we have mortar and bricks. Hence: *But they were rebellious at the sea, even at the Red Sea.*

(Exodus Rabbah 24:1)

THE MIDRASH

By Judah is God known. (Psalm 76:2)

Rabbi Judah ben Rabbi Il'ai expounded: When Israel stood by the Red Sea the tribes stood contending with each other, one saying, "I will go in first," and the other saying, "I will go in first." At that moment Nahshon [of the tribe of Judah] leapt into the waves of the sea and waded in. In allusion to him David said, *Save me, O God; for the waters are come in even unto the soul* (Psalm 69:2). Said the Holy One, the blessed One, to Moses: "My beloved is drowning in the sea and you stand praying! Speak to the children of Israel, that they go forward" (Exodus 14:15). This explains: *By Judah is God known.* **For this reason the Holy One, the blessed One, made great the name of Nahshon in Israel.**

(Numbers Rabbah 13:4)

These midrashim address the question of what happened when the people of Israel encountered the Red Sea. Fresh out of slavery and afraid, they saw the waters raging before them. Behind them were the Egyptians, Pharaoh's warriors with all their chariots and horses. The people of Israel could not go forward because of the sea, and they could not retreat because of the advancing Egyptian army. The rabbis imagine that they must have quarreled about the proper course of action.

Perhaps there was a contest among the tribes, each wishing to have the distinction of being the first in the sea. Rabbi Judah ben Rabbi Il'ai imagines a great deal of talking and boasting but little action, until one person, Nahshon from the tribe of Judah, tires of all the bickering and posturing and musters the courage to leap into the waves.

More likely, as the midrash from Exodus Rabbah suggests, the people were reluctant to walk into the waters before knowing what would happen, with no guarantee of safety. After all, how could they know that a miracle would occur, that the sea would split? Reason would have dictated surrender, risking Egypt's wrath rather than certain death by drowning.

Such quarrels might have mirrored similar arguments in the rabbis' own day concerning how to act in dangerous times. The risks for independence have been equally treacherous in later generations. In fact, it is easy to see reflections in these midrashim of the disputes and posturing among politicians of our own time over how to respond to perilous threats.

While the leaders of the tribes are debating about the fitting response to the crisis before them, one individual takes action. Nahshon ben Amminadab from the tribe of Judah walks into the waters. It is said that it was not until the waters reached his nose that the sea split. So the midrash understands the verse from Psalms, *by Judah is God known*, to mean that God is made known through the deeds of Nahshon, a member of the tribe of Judah; God is made present through the courageous acts of human beings.

The midrash goes further in emphasizing the role of human responsibility in changing the course of history, in bringing redemption. It sees Moses standing at the sea at the head of all the people of Israel, praying, calling out to God to save him. And God responds, not by immediately splitting the waters so the people can walk on dry land and escape the pursuing Egyptians, but, surprisingly, by castigating Moses for lengthening his prayer at such a critical time. When Moses wonders what else he could possibly do but pray, God responds simply, "Go forward." In other words, God is saying, "I will be with you, but don't depend on Me for a miracle. To believe in Me is to act without fear as if everything depends upon you, because it does." Nahshon is the first to respond to the divine command, to take the risk necessary for freedom, and God's presence is manifest in his act of heroism. Prayer has its place, but it is not a substitute for courage and responsible action.

But there is another source of rebellion at the sea. The rabbis question why the verse in Psalms says that the people "were rebellious at the sea," and then repeats, "at the Red Sea." Since no words are considered superfluous in the original text, there must have been a particular purpose or meaning behind this repetition.

According to the midrash, the first rebellion was the one we have just discussed. All the people except Nahshon refused to walk into the sea. The second rebellion was of a different nature. It was a result not of fear but of ingratitude. Even as the sea split and the people were able to walk through the waters, some still complained.

The midrash tells us that the tribes of Reuben and Simeon could not see the miracle that had just occurred. The sea may have split, but they saw only the clay that formed at the bottom of the sea. Now they had to trek through mud, just as in Egypt they had to make bricks out of mud. For Reuben and Simeon there was no difference. Freedom didn't feel all that distinct from slavery.

The tribes of Reuben and Simeon saw what they expected to see: the hardship of that improbable journey. And they were most likely accurate in their assessment. After all, it couldn't have been all that pleasant to walk with a group of men, women, and children, some so young they needed to be carried, some so old they required assistance. They may not have had all that much to take with them, but whatever they brought had to weigh heavily on their shoulders so that their backs ached. Their feet were caked with wet earth, their only shoes were ruined, and the hems of their clothes were soaked with mud.

Reuben and Simeon gave an accurate description, but not a correct one. Something extraordinary had just happened, but their eyes were closed to the miracle. Nahshon realized it; he leaped, eyes open, into the waters of the sea. Miriam saw it; she lifted her tambourine and danced. Perhaps the rabbis were attempting to encourage the people of their own time to look beyond the daily drudgery of their situation to recognize God's presence in their midst, to find the courage of Nahshon and the joy of Miriam.

A PERSONAL REFLECTION

When I think of Nahshon finding the courage and faith to walk into the waters of the sea without knowing if they would split, I think of my father. I first learned about that kind of faith in my father's arms.

Every summer when I was young I would go to the New Jersey shore with my family. Our family would rent a house, and spend warm days on the beach, and lazy evenings strolling the boardwalk. My dad would come and spend weekends with us. Suntan lotion, salt, and sweet frozen custard were the smells and tastes of summer.

I especially loved the ocean. I delighted in venturing far out to try to catch a wave and ride it back to shore. Then one day I was toppled by an unusually large wave, and the strong pull of the tide made it hard for me to regain my balance. For what seemed like forever, I felt trapped. By the time I managed to reach the surface, I was out of breath and trembling. I recovered, but I was frightened by the experience.

When my father joined our family at the beach that weekend, he noticed that something about me had changed. I no longer plunged into the ocean, but seemed content to play where the water barely lapped at my ankles. My father coaxed me to join him farther from the shore, but I declined.

It was then that, despite my fear and persistent protests, he took my hand and led me out with him into the ocean. When a large wave threatened, he lifted me up and carried me in his arms. He never let go until I once again learned to love the waves.

It is ironic that my father had short arms. All the long-sleeved shirts I bought him for birthday and Father's

Day gifts had to be adjusted. But in those arms, more than in all my theology textbooks, I learned about God and courage and faith.

In the Bible, the extended arms of Pharaoh's daughter save Moses from the waters of the Nile, and Moses' uplifted arms teach the people about faith. When Moses raises his arms, no enemy can triumph over Israel. Nahshon walks straight into the sea, enabling a frightened people to trust the waters that become their passage to freedom.

In our own lives, the arms that carry us, lift us up, and embrace us teach us the most about bravery, trust, and faith. In the arms of a parent, a loved one, a friend, we experience the outstretched arms of God. I think of God as the arms that carry me over the waves until I am able to walk on my own. I think of God as the arms that hold me and coax and prod me to do much more than I ever imagined I could.

WHERE DO YOU SEE YOURSELF IN THE STORY?

What might you have said when you reached the sea?

Are there times when you have been more like Reuben and Simeon, times when you have been more like Nahshon?

From where do your deepest lessons of faith come?

I Will Call You Batya, Daughter of God
Loving the Stranger

Women in the Bible often have neither a name nor a voice. They somehow fit into someone else's story, but rarely is the story about them. Yet in the second chapter of Exodus, women direct the narrative flow. Women defy Pharaoh's murderous edict, a woman gives birth to a boy, his sister watches over him, and a daughter of Pharaoh saves him from certain death in the Nile. Without these women there is no Moses and no liberation.

The rabbis create midrash in their attempt to understand the Egyptian princess, to give her a name and a story. What is striking is not just the powerful part that they imagine a woman playing in this salvation account, but the startling role of an outsider, a person of a different class and faith. On the banks of the Nile, the daughter of Pharaoh and the young slave Miriam meet in a groundbreaking interfaith encounter, and the result is redemptive.

Sometimes we are like Moses and Miriam in the story, in need of an extended hand. Will we take the hand of the stranger, our presumed enemy? And sometimes we are like Pharaoh's daughter, in a position to offer help. When, where, and to whom will we extend our hand?

The daughter of Pharaoh came down to bathe in the river while her maidens walked walked along the Nile. (Exodus 2:5)

She came down to bathe in order to cleanse herself from the idols of her father's palace. *And her maidens walked along.* Rabbi Yohanan said, The expression "walked" here means walking to meet death, as it is said, *Behold, I am at the point of death* (Genesis 25:32). Her maidens said to her: "Your Highness, it is the general rule that when a king makes a decree, his own family will obey, even if everyone else transgresses it, but you are flagrantly disobeying your father's command." Whereupon the angel Gabriel came and smote them to the ground. And Pharaoh's daughter sent her maid [*amata*] to fetch the basket. . . . Rabbi Judah and Rabbi Nehemiah discuss this. One says the word *amata* means "her hand" and the other "her handmaid." . . . According to the one who thinks that it means "her handmaid," Gabriel must have spared one maid when he smote the others, because it is not right for a princess to remain unattended. . . . According to him who says that it means "her hand," why does it not explicitly say "her hand [*yada*]"? . . . The word *amata* is used on purpose because her arms were lengthened.

(Exodus Rabbah 1:23)

When the child grew up, she [Miriam] *brought him to Pharaoh's daughter, who made him her son. And she called him Moses, explaining, I drew him out of the water.* (Exodus 2:10)

From here you can infer how great is the reward of those who perform kind acts; for although Moses had many names, the name by which he is known in the Torah is the one which Batya, the daughter of Pharaoh, called him, and even God called him by no other name.

(Exodus Rabbah 1:26)

And these are the sons of Batya, the daughter of Pharaoh. . . . (1 Chronicles 4:18)

Rabbi Joshua of Siknin said in the name of Rabbi Levi: The Holy One, the blessed One, said to Batya, the daughter of Pharaoh: "Moses was not your son, yet you called him your son; you, too, though you are not My daughter, yet I will call you Batya, the daughter of God."

(Leviticus Rabbah 1:3)

The rabbis wonder what would bring Pharaoh's daughter down to the river to bathe. They assume that a woman of her standing in the Egyptian court would have the servants prepare her bath in the palace. Why would she drag her attendants to the river where the common folk wash? The poor and the slave come to the river's edge to bathe, but certainly not the princess.

The rabbis imagine the princess as set apart from the rest of the royal court. She is not an idol worshiper like her father. The waters of the Nile are seen as having spiritual cleansing qualities, and she seeks them out. But though attendants accompany Pharaoh's daughter, the midrash doubts that they are in agreement with her.

Rabbi Yohanan relates the phrase "and her maidens walked along" to a verse in Genesis that actually refers to Esau, who "walks" up to Jacob after returning from hunting. Esau is famished, "at the point of death." The two narratives are inherently unrelated, but the midrash suggests a tenuous linguistic connection. Assuredly, the rabbi imagines, the servants must have feared that by walking with, that is, by serving the princess who was defying the Pharaoh's order, they might be jeopardizing their own lives. Pharaoh has commanded that every newborn Hebrew son be cast into the Nile. The servants of Pharaoh's daughter recognize that she has dragged them to the river to counter her father's heartless decree.

The midrash imagines a conversation between the daughter of Pharaoh and her attendants, who question her decision to transgress the law of the land, especially since her father is its source. God has a stake in this argument, and God leaves nothing to chance. An angel, Gabriel, is sent to strike down the servants, in effect to assist the princess in her endeavor.

The Bible says that when Pharaoh's daughter saw the basket among the reeds, she sent her slave girl to fetch it (Exodus 2:5). The Hebrew word *amata* can mean "her handmaiden" or her "handbreadth." Playing with this Hebrew peculiarity, Rabbi Judah and Rabbi Nehemiah wonder whether it was the handmaiden whom Gabriel spares or whether it is the princess's hand that is extended beyond its normal length to fetch Moses's basket.

It is Pharaoh's daughter who gives the child his name. Other midrashim imagine that Miriam, his sister, and Yocheved, his mother, also choose names for their brother and son. After all, the rabbis suspect that the naming of the child would not be left to a stranger, a member of the Egyptian court, the daughter of the Pharaoh who so oppressed the people of Israel. Our midrash questions why the name the Egyptian princess gives the child is the one by which he becomes known. It attributes this choice to the generosity, grace, and loving-kindness that Pharaoh's daughter shows the child. God rewards the Egyptian woman for her selfless act.

The book of Exodus understands the name *Moses* to derive from the Hebrew *I drew him out of the water* (Exodus 2:10). However, modern scholars suggest that the name *Moses* derives from the Egyptian word meaning "son." Many of the great Pharaohs contain a form of "moses" as part of their names, for example, Thutmoses (son of Thoth) and Ramoses (son of Ra).

✳ ✳ ✳ ✳ ✳ ✳ ✳ ✳ ✳ ✳

It is not uncommon in the Bible to find that women have no names and no stories. The story of Noah and the Flood is an important narrative in the book of Genesis. We learn something about Noah's character, what he does to save the world from total annihilation. We read about his construction of the ark, and we are told about the vineyard he plants when he leaves the ark after the flood waters have subsided. However, we know nothing about Noah's wife. She has neither a name nor a story. Midrash often fills in those blanks and provides a name and a story.

In the case of Pharaoh's daughter, the midrash calls her Batya, which means daughter (*bat*) of God (*Yah*). Imagine calling the child of your archenemy the daughter of God. Rabbi Joshua explains that Pharaoh's daughter called Moses her son when in fact he was not her son, but the son of a Hebrew woman. Her altruistic and magnanimous love for a slave child, a child whose death has been decreed by her own father, causes God to choose a name for the princess that will trump her Egyptian given name, which midrash records as Thermutis.

* * *

Other midrashim wonder how it was possible for Batya to convince her father that this child drawn from the Nile was not in fact a Hebrew child. How could Pharaoh have accepted this baby in his home, a slave child he had ordered killed, if he believed his daughter had brought him to the palace in defiance of his edict? It was bad enough that the midwives, Shifrah and Puah, had thwarted Pharaoh's command to kill all the Hebrew boys at birth. They had claimed that the Hebrew women were like animals in the field and delivered before the midwives could arrive to assist them. It would have been insufferable for a rebellious child of his own to thwart his diabolical plan. How then did Batya succeed in placating her father and winning his approval to allow the child to grow up at the palace?

One midrash suggests that Batya feigned pregnancy for some time before she brought the baby to her father's home. Another text imagines that the princess played into her father's belief system and told him that the exceedingly beautiful child she called Moses was a gift of the sacred river, the Nile.

The rabbis wonder what became of the Egyptian princess during the tenth plague when the angel of death visited the homes of Egypt and killed all the firstborn Egyptian children. The rabbinic narrative notes that none of the plagues visited upon Egypt because of Pharaoh's hardheartedness afflicted Batya. Although she was the firstborn of her mother, she remained safe from any harm.

Another midrash actually imagines Batya traveling with the people of Israel out of Egypt and eventually marrying a Hebrew man, Caleb, from the tribe of Judah.

Caleb was one of the two scouts who returned from scouting out the land of Israel and offered a positive assessment of the people's ability to enter the Promised Land. The midrashim hold this Egyptian woman in such high regard that they not only call her the daughter of God, but even envision her as one of the very few to be accorded the distinction of entering Paradise alive.

A PERSONAL REFLECTION

I am always searching for women's names. Who was Lot's wife, a person usually known only as a model of disobedience, her pillar of salt an eternal symbol of female weakness and rebellion? What if we imagine that when she fled Sodom and Gomorrah she turned back, not out of disobedience to God's command, but out of compassion for her daughters who were following her? The pillar of salt was her tears. The rabbis give her a name, Idit.

Who was Noah's wife, and what did she do cooped up in the ark for so many days and nights? In the midrash she has a name, Naamah.

And why was she called Naamah? Because her deeds were "ne'emim," pleasing.
(Genesis Rabbah 23:3)

What if we imagined her story?

Names are powerful. They represent an individual's essence. In the Bible, when a person's character changes, he or she is given a new name. Jacob acquires the name *Israel* after he struggles with the angel and wrests a blessing. His night encounter transforms him and makes him into a new person, an individual capable of leading the Israelites.

In Jewish tradition, the name of the evil villain Haman, who plots to annihilate the entire Jewish community, is blotted out. During the festival of Purim, when the book of Esther is recited, loud noisemakers known as groggers drown out Haman's name whenever it is read aloud. With large fanfare we seek to wipe out this ignoble name. Yet with little or no fanfare, we have been quietly blotting out the names of noble women for generations.

What would happen, I wondered, if I listened to the silences in the text and gave name and story to women who were mentioned in the Bible, but whose narratives did not exist? What would happen if I imagined the characters on the margins whose only purpose was to propel someone else's story? What if they became the subject of the narrative and got to tell their own story?

The rabbis called Pharaoh's daughter Batya, daughter of God. More than just the woman who conveniently finds her way to the Nile at precisely the right moment and saves Moses from drowning in the river, she is a human being caught between her father's court, her country's law, and her own sense of compassion and justice. Her courage and daring are matched by her cleverness and loyalty.

It must have taken some convincing for the daughter of the ruler of all Egypt to persuade her handmaidens to accompany her to the Nile, to mingle with the commoners who went there regularly to bathe. Pharaoh had hired the servants to protect his only daughter, Thermutis, to shield her from the ugliness of slavery he had imposed on the people of Israel. "She is too soft-hearted," he would say.

I imagine Thermutis was able to persuade her father that the god of the Nile had called to her. She must have insisted that the holy waters of the sacred river were required to bring peace to her restless soul. Thermutis knew that Pharaoh would not be able to resist that argument, but it was not the real reason for her desire to travel to the river's bank. She knew of her father's decree that all boys born to Hebrew women be drowned in the Nile, and she did not approve.

When she reached the riverbank she saw a basket drifting just beyond her grasp. She asked her handmaids to help her retrieve it, but they were afraid. "Assuredly, there is a Hebrew infant in this basket. Pharaoh will punish us if we disobey his orders." Thermutis's servants tried to restrain her, fearing for their own safety.

Thermutis lay down in the wet earth along the Nile and extended her arms as far as they would reach, grabbing hold of a corner of the basket and pulling it toward her. Just as she had expected, when she opened the basket, she saw a baby boy. When the infant began to cry, she lifted him up and cradled him in her arms.

"If Pharaoh decrees the death of all Hebrew sons, then you will be *my* son. I will call you Moses, son, son of Thermutis, daughter of Pharaoh. I will tell my father that the god of the Nile gave you to me as a son, and he will listen to me, and I will keep you safe." Thermutis spoke softly to the child as if he could understand. Her handmaidens kept their distance so as not to be implicated in their mistress's ruse.

I imagine that Moses came to love Thermutis as a mother. Even when he had to leave the palace, he would never have forgotten her. He must have gone to see her during all those return visits to Pharaoh when he and Aaron sought freedom for their people. I see her as Moses's advocate, pleading with her father, plague after plague, to soften his heart and let the people of Israel go. It might have been not only God but Thermutis who gave Moses the courage to go to Pharaoh in the first place. And when Pharaoh hardened his heart, he must have broken hers.

In the middle of the night when the tenth plague swept through Egypt, it must have been Moses who saved Thermutis, the firstborn of one of Pharaoh's wives, from death. And under cover of night, I imagine she went with him, one Egyptian among the Israelites who crossed the sea. When she saw Moses lift his arm over the waters, she called out, "My son!" And God called back, "Batya, my daughter!"

It must have been Batya who moved Moses to teach his people to love the stranger as she had saved him and loved him, a stranger in the land of Egypt.

WHERE DO YOU SEE YOURSELF IN THE STORY?

Have you ever felt like the handmaidens in the midrash, afraid to defy the rules even when you question them? When have you felt like Pharaoh's daughter, caught between your own compassion and the laws of the land?

Imagine a conversation between Miriam and Pharaoh's daughter when they meet at the river Nile. Think of other interfaith encounters that have the potential to yield a story of redemption.

Suppose that Pharaoh's daughter and Moses have a conversation when he returns to the palace to ask for his people's freedom. What would they say to one another? What might Pharaoh's daughter say to her father?

God Teaches Adam to Make Fire
Getting through the Night

here are many stories throughout history and across cultures about how human beings acquired the ability to make fire. In the following midrash, fire is a gift that provides not only warmth and light but also hope. The rabbis were able to imagine Adam's desperation when the sun set, because they had faced it themselves. There were moments in their own experience when they had to doubt their ability to survive. They knew this fear as leaders of a people under foreign rule and in exile, and as individuals subject to personal loss and pain.

When the light of their outside world grew faint, they searched for a way to kindle an inner light. The story of Adam's first night gave them a way to talk about their own dark nights and to find a way to the morning. If we listen deeply enough, it may do the same for us.

THE MIDRASH

And God blessed the seventh day. . . . (Genesis 2:3)

With what did God bless the seventh day? With light. When the sun set on the night of

the Sabbath, that light continued to function.
. . . But when the sun sank at the termination of
the Sabbath, darkness began to set in. Adam was
terrified, thinking: *Surely, the darkness shall envelop
me* (Psalm 139:11). . . .

What did God do for him? God made Adam
find two flints that he struck against each other;
light came forth and Adam uttered a blessing
over it.

(Genesis Rabbah 11:2)

The rabbis wondered what special blessing belonged
to the holiest of days, the weekly Sabbath. One
rabbi imagined that the blessing consisted of the
double portion of manna given only on the evening
of the seventh day, so that people would not need to
gather food on the Sabbath. Another suggested that the
Sabbath was blessed by the special garments worn on
that day. Still another offered that the blessing had to do
with a unique spice, unlike any other condiment, that
gave the delicious taste to all food served on Shabbat.

But the midrashic tradition centering on this portion
of Scripture provides a fourth intriguing reason that
the Sabbath was blessed. God created man on the sixth
day, but, according to the midrash, the first time Adam
experienced darkness was at the end of the seventh
day, the Sabbath. Even though, the midrash says, Adam

sinned before the beginning of Shabbat, God still chose to honor the seventh day with a special light.

The rabbis imagine that the particular blessing of the Sabbath is the light that shone through Adam's first night until the end of Shabbat. But by the end of the seventh day, the light ceased and Adam grew fearful. Perhaps he despaired and believed that there was nothing he could do to change the course of events. His sin had brought about the end of the world. Having never witnessed a sunrise, how would Adam know that the sunset was not, in fact, the end of all life? Surely without the sun's light and heat the world would grow cold and life would cease. How could Adam get through the hours of darkness believing that light would never grace his world again? It was then that, according to the midrash, God taught Adam to make fire to help him get through the night.

The midrash is addressing a much more profound concern than how fire came into being or how Adam managed to survive the first night. It is a narrative about the dark, the times we have despaired because of what we have done or what nature or people have done to us. It is about those moments when we are afraid that the sun won't rise again, and it seems that there is nothing we can do.

There is no suggestion in the midrash that God will change the order of nature. God does not make the sun appear in the midst of the night, nor does God stop the sun from setting again and again. Rather, the rabbis suggest, we ourselves have the ability to somehow make light even in the deepest dark of night. When God taught Adam to make fire, God gave him the gift of resiliency, the power to meet the challenge of the night without giving up on the day, and the ability to go on with life.

A PERSONAL REFLECTION

Once it seemed that the sun had set for the Jewish people. During that long night of the Holocaust, it was hard to believe that the sun would ever rise again. Yet some people in the midst of that horrific tragedy somehow found enough light to carry them through the darkness.

I am reminded of a friend of mine who is a Holocaust survivor. His name is Mike. He was liberated from Auschwitz with his mother when he was five years old. No one else in his immediate family survived. His wife, Judy, and I are best friends. We shared the joys and trials of motherhood, commiserated about working and raising families, but rarely spoke of how Mike's experiences influenced their lives.

All I knew was that when Mike's mother came to visit, Judy would tell me that her mother-in-law collected the leftovers from the kitchen and hid them in the drawers in her room. She must have believed that the time might come again when food would be scarce and she would need her stash of food to survive. So I guess I knew that Mike's life had to have changed because of his experience, but it wasn't obvious how.

Over time, Mike told me more of his story. He couldn't remember any of his years in Auschwitz. All he could relate was what his mother told him. Unlike his brother, he was able to survive because he was so tiny. His mom could hide him whenever the concentration camp guards came for inspections. It was hard to believe that Mike was once a small and scrawny child. He loved to eat and constantly struggled with a weight problem. Even though he didn't remember the camp, I suppose his experience there led him to eat whatever was available whenever it was available. It was once a matter of survival.

Mike did remember the refugee camps after the war. Mostly he recalled how terrible they were. One day he and his mother decided to return to their hometown in Zharki, Poland. They had once owned a home there, and they hoped that the neighbors had saved some of their possessions. His mom had buried some jewelry and other valuables in their yard for safekeeping. But when Mike and his mother went to dig up the few precious items they had buried, they found no jewelry, no silver, not even a single family photograph. Not one picture of parents or grandparents, nieces or nephews remained, not one picture of Mike's father or brother— all who had perished in the camps. When the family was herded together with other Jewish people in the city and put on trains for camps and extermination, the neighbors must have ransacked the house. The people of Zharki never thought anyone would return.

Mike and his mother found only one reminder of days gone by—a small silver kiddush cup. This precious cup had once held sweet wine to usher in the Sabbath and holy days. It once was lifted to mark moments of celebration in a toast to light and life—*l'chaim*. Now it was all that was left of a dark past that had gone up in smoke. And there seemed no reason to fill it. There was nothing sweet or good to celebrate. Yes, Mike and his mother had survived against great odds, but the night had not lifted. Life was hard and sad, and there was too much death.

Mike brought the kiddush cup to America. He and his wife, Judy, had four children. They were the kindest, most giving parents you could know. And they were the best of friends—always there for you, no matter what.

My husband and I had the privilege of officiating at the weddings of three of Mike and Judy's four children. Standing under the wedding canopy with bride and groom, I lifted that silver kiddush cup. I handed it to the new couple filled with sweet wine. Now it was time to say a blessing, to celebrate. Here were lives that were not meant to be. Here was the future that was supposed to have been eradicated. The kiddush cup was to have been a piece in a museum of an extinct people. But it wasn't. It was here in the hands of a bride and groom, and it held the promise of a sweet future.

When I held that cup at each wedding ceremony and recited the traditional blessing over wine, I thought of how God had taught Adam to make fire to get through the night. Against all odds, Mike had created a small fire. Like the two flints that Adam rubbed together, Mike and his mother had kindled a spark, and then he and his wife had kindled another. Working together, these brave people created enough light to last until the sun finally rose.

That night of the wedding of Mike and Judy's first child, we filled the empty kiddush cup with wine and we toasted *l'chaim*, "To life!" A new light came forth, and we all pronounced the blessing.

WHERE DO YOU SEE YOURSELF IN THE STORY?

Think of a time when you felt afraid like Adam, when you believed the sun had set and would not rise again.

What helped you get through the night? What was the fire that gave you light?

How would you bless that light?

Where do you think Mike and his mother found the strength to go on and bless life?

What Made Miriam Dance and Akiba Laugh?
Making the Sound of Hope

Amedeo Modigliani was one of Italy's best-known modernist portrait painters. A subject of one of his paintings once asked why he had painted him with one eye open and the other eye closed. The artist answered, "With one eye you see the world; with the other you see yourself." And that is exactly how the rabbis read the Bible. With one eye they saw the world around them, with all its difficulties and joys, and with the other they saw the human soul, with all its frailty and audacity.

In this chapter we join the rabbis as they imagine what enabled Miriam to see beyond Pharaoh's death decrees, and what empowers the human heart in difficult circumstances to rise above a pessimistic view of the present to an optimistic vision of the future. We are not always in control of the world we see around us, but how we interpret that world depends on our other eye, the eye that sees ourselves. Do we approach life with resignation or with confidence, with distrust or with hope, with fear or with courage? The following midrashim open our inner eye and help us realize that most often we see just what we expect.

THE MIDRASH

A certain man of the house of Levi went and he took [married] a daughter of Levi. (Exodus 2:1)

Amram [the father of Moses] was at that time the head of the Sanhedrin, and when Pharaoh decreed, "If it is a boy, kill him," Amram said that it was useless for the Israelites to beget children. Immediately he ceased to have intercourse with his wife, Jochebed. He even divorced her though she was already three months pregnant. Then [following his example] all the Israelites also divorced their wives. Amram's daughter, Miriam, said to him, "Your decree of divorce is more severe than that of Pharaoh; for Pharaoh decreed only concerning the male children, while your decree concerns male and female alike. Besides, Pharaoh is wicked, so it is doubtful whether or not his decree will be fulfilled, but you are righteous and your decree will be fulfilled." So Amram married his wife again and his example was followed by all the Israelites who remarried their wives.

(Exodus Rabbah 1:13)

A certain man of the house of Levi went and he took [married] a daughter of Levi. . . . (Exodus 2:1)

Where did he go? Rabbi Judah the son of Rabbi Zebina said: He followed his daughter's advice. It was taught: Amram was the leading man of his generation; *and took [to wife] a daughter of Levi.* It does not say "he took her back" but *he took,* proving, said Rabbi Judah the son of Zebina, that he went through a marriage ceremony with her. He placed her on the bridal litter, Miriam and Aaron dancing before them and the angels saying: *As a joyful mother of children* (Psalm 113:9).

(Exodus Rabbah 1:19)

And his sister stood at a distance, to learn what would befall him. (Exodus 2:4)

Why did Miriam stand at a distance? Rabbi Amram in the name of Rab said: Because Miriam prophesied, "My mother is destined to give birth to a son who will save Israel." When the house was flooded with light at the birth of Moses, her father arose and kissed her head and said: "My daughter, your prophecy has been fulfilled." . . . But now that she was casting him [Moses] into the river, her mother struck her on the head saying: "My daughter, what about the prophecy?" This is why it says: *And his sister stood at a distance,* to know what would become of her prophecy. (Exodus Rabbah 1:22)

These first two midrashim are trying to make sense of the first verse of the second chapter of Exodus. It is clear that "a certain man of the house of Levi" refers to Moses' father, Amram, and "a daughter of Levi" refers to Moses' mother, Yocheved. But why would the text speak of the marriage of Amram and Yocheved at this point? Weren't they already married? After all, they had borne two children, Aaron and Miriam. Remember—because there is nothing inconsequential in the biblical text, not even the order of chapter and verse, the rabbis seek to find significance in this odd chronological placement of Amram and Yocheved's marriage. In doing so they develop another narrative to fill in the missing explanation: they imagine a second wedding.

When Pharaoh decreed the death of all male children, the people of Israel despaired. The future held only the promise of death, and there seemed no reason to continue to bear children. So Amram, a respected community leader, decided to divorce his wife and discontinue sexual relations. Following Amram's example, all the Israelite men did the same. But Miriam questioned the wisdom of their decision. After all, Pharaoh had decreed the death of all the male children but not the females. Amram's action would mean the loss of female children as well, assuring the end of the people of Israel. Amram recognized his daughter's wisdom and remarried Yocheved in a public ceremony so that his wedding would serve as an example to all the men of Israel. They followed his lead, remarried their wives, and secured the future.

These midrashim are not just simple explanations of a perplexing verse. The rabbis are also addressing the psychology of despair and hope. Amram sees reality as it is. The people are powerless slaves. Pharaoh has decreed the death of a new generation of sons. Reason tells him to give up; there is no possibility for a future. Why continue to suffer?

Miriam sees what is, but also what can be. She knows the same set of facts, but she does not stop there. She envisions what can be, the possibility of a different future. Reason may counsel her to give up, but hope and imagination tell her to go on. It is she who prophesies the birth of Moses and anticipates in him a redeemer of her people. Amram and Yocheved rejoice with her only for a moment. When they place Moses in the Nile, they return to their view of reality. They are angry with Miriam for giving them false hope. Now they are certain that Moses will die in the Nile and with him, their daughter's prophecy. But despite the foreboding circumstances, Miriam refuses to give in to despair. She remains vigilant, guarding Moses from a distance. She doesn't abandon her brother; she does not relinquish her hope of what still can be.

Midrashim such as these were written during the period of Roman rule over the Jews. They echo the concerns of the generation in which they were written. Reeling under the weight of Roman oppression, the Jewish people had every reason to despair, to give up hoping for a future time of sovereignty. There was no reason to believe that the political situation would change. But the rabbis suggest a different view. They don't stop at oppression; they look beyond the present to the future.

The Talmud relates a narrative with a similar message regarding the destruction of the Second Temple:

> Rabbi Akiba was walking with his colleagues, Rabbi Gamaliel, Rabbi Eliezer, and Rabbi Joshua, on the Temple mount that was in ruins. All four rabbis saw a little fox run about on the ruins of the Temple mount, on the place where the Holy of Holies once stood. Three of the four began weeping, but Rabbi Akiba laughed.

> "Why do you weep?" Rabbi Akiba asked his colleagues.

> The three answered, "Because the place of the Temple is now the place of the fox."

Then the three rabbis asked Rabbi Akiba, "Why do you laugh, seeing all this destruction, seeing that the people are gone and only the fox remains?"

Rabbi Akiba answered, "Because just as the prophet foretold the destruction of Jerusalem, so the prophet foretold the future restoration of the city. Now that Jerusalem has been destroyed, the first prophecy fulfilled, we know that the second prophecy, the rebuilding of Jerusalem, will also be fulfilled."

(BT Makkot 24b)

Akiba sees beyond the present reality, the devastation and desolation of Jerusalem in ruins. Like Miriam, he envisions an alternate reality. The way things are is not the way things need to be. Akiba doesn't stop with destruction; he doesn't accept the foxes running about a barren Jerusalem as the final scenario. He doesn't give up hope. He imagines another possibility, another reality.

The rabbis recognize that such vision is necessary also in times of plenty. They teach that the future always requires imagination.

THE MIDRASH

When you enter the land of Israel, you shall plant all kinds of trees for food. . . . (Leviticus 19:23)

The Holy One, the blessed One said to Israel, "Even if you find the land full of all good things, do not say, 'We will sit and not plant'; rather be diligent in planting. . . . Just as you came and found trees planted by others, you must plant for your children."

A person must not say, "I am old, how many years will I live? Why should I stand and exert myself for others? Tomorrow I will die." You must not excuse yourself from planting. As you found trees, plant more, even if you are old.

(Midrash Tanhuma, Kedoshim 8)

The midrash asks: If the land is flowing with milk and honey, if we have enough trees for our own use, why should we expend energy in planting new trees when we may not live to enjoy their fruit or their shade?

Along similar lines, the Talmud tells the story of an old man who was planting a carob tree when a king rode by. "Old man," the king called out, "how old are you?" "Seventy years, your majesty," the man replied. "How many years will it take before that tree will bear fruit?" the king asked. "Perhaps seventy years," the man answered. Mockingly, the king went on, "Do you really expect to eat of the fruit of that tree?" "Of course not," the man said, "but just as I found fruit trees when I was born, so do I plant trees that future generations may eat from them" (Taanit 23a).

A woman in my congregation, the mother of triplets, was diagnosed with breast cancer when her children were only one year old. She had loved gardening and hoped to plant a rose garden in her yard. But when she received the dreaded news of her malignancy, she told her husband that there was no reason for them to buy rose bushes; she doubted she would ever see them bloom. They bought the roses despite her illness. They planted them anyway. She fertilized, watered, and weeded. She saw them bloom.

Her children were eleven years old when she died. For a while, no one had any interest in the roses. Untended, the garden began to fill with weeds. Just a few hearty roses survived the neglect, but they desperately needed pruning. After all, it had been the woman's rose garden, and she was no longer there to care for it. The family was busy with more immediate concerns—school assignments, cooking, cleaning, and bills, not to mention coping with the emptiness. There seemed no reason to buy more bushes, to plant more roses. Yet one day the husband bought some anyway. He and the children put on gloves, and they began to dig in the earth. They planted and fertilized, watered and weeded, and the garden bloomed again.

That rose garden reminds me of Rabbi Akiba and his laughter in the face of loss, and the mother's roses and the rabbi's laughter both call to mind Miriam's dance and song.

When the people of Israel escaped Egyptian bondage and crossed the Sea of Reeds, the book of Exodus tells us: *Then Miriam the prophetess, Aaron's sister, took a timbrel in her hand, and all the women went out after her in dance with timbrels. And Miriam chanted for them* (Exodus 15:20–21). Her dance, like Akiba's laughter and a mother's roses, contains the promise of what yet can be.

A PERSONAL REFLECTION

Miriam danced. And I wonder, would I have danced? There were all those years of oppression, slavery, and nothing going right. She was the older sister, but her brother, Moses, received all the acclaim. She watched in the bulrushes to insure his safety and did everything in her power to save him, but he took the lead in the Exodus drama. Her imagination saved a whole generation from disaster, but no one seemed to notice. Moses gave us the Torah, tradition says, and the words echo through the generations to my own day. But what about the teaching that Miriam gave us?

And yet Miriam danced. And I wonder, could I have danced? Caught between nature's fury and human rage, the people of Israel had to make an act of faith—or was it foolishness?—to walk through the waters. The movies make the trek to freedom look like an easy stroll. But what about all the mud and seaweed, the women in long skirts carrying babies, and everyone with the wrong shoes? Miriam's sandals couldn't have survived the crossing. I imagine she discarded them along with any other excess baggage. She kept only her tambourine—a strange choice. What use could she have imagined for a musical instrument in the desert? Better a jug of water, I think.

And still Miriam danced. And I wonder, would I have joined her? She had to have questioned God. Why allow so many years of slavery? Why harden Pharaoh's heart? She couldn't have thought it was God who ordained it all and still sing praises.

And yet Miriam danced. She might have complained about the difficulties, despaired about the unknown tomorrow. Many who made the Exodus journey did just that. "It was better in Egypt," they said, "better than drowning in the sea or dying of thirst and hunger in the desert."

Yet Miriam lifted her tambourine and made the sound of hope. And the people heard it carried in the wind, singing in the waves. So Miriam danced, and all the people joined her.

I think that I will dance with them.

WHERE DO YOU SEE YOURSELF IN THE STORY?

Think of a time when you felt like Amram and Yocheved, ready to give up on the future.

When are you more like Moses's parents, and when are you more like Miriam? Do you tend to be more like Akiba or more like his colleagues?

When reason would tell you to give up and give in, what gives you hope? What keeps you planting?

Would you dance with Miriam? What is your tambourine?

Conclusion:
What Can Midrash Do?
Learning to Dance While Standing Still

I want to leave you with more than a collection of reflections on ancient midrashim. I want to leave you with the understanding that midrash can be a way of entering into the biblical tradition that is ours as much as it was our ancestors'.

Many midrashim attempt to explain the light that was created on the first day of creation before the sun and the moon. In the first chapter of Genesis we are told that God said, *Let there be light. And there was light.* But it is not until the fourth day of creation that God creates the greater light to rule the day and the lesser night to rule the night. The rabbis explain that this first light was a sacred primordial light, brighter by far than the sun and moon. Some say that when Adam and Eve sinned, God took away that light in order to save it for the righteous in the world to come. Others suggest that it was hidden in the Torah. Still others imagine that, though the light was concealed, it still exists in the world and renews daily the works of creation.

Sometimes midrash helps us make sense of our feelings, gives us words when we have none. When my son and daughter-in-law became parents for the first time, I wanted desperately to find words to give voice to the joyful tears. To see your child hold his own child—this is a moment whose delight is hard to describe.

And in those first days of the child's life, I recalled the midrash about the first light. The idea of a light, neither sun or moon, so hidden that it was rarely seen, had always seemed a bit strange and fanciful. Not until I became a grandparent did I understand what the midrash meant. You stand in a chain of the generations. You watch your children with their own child, and you see where that primordial light is hidden. You actually hold that sacred light in your arms. It is why you find your eyes filling up with tears.

During the days that followed the birth of our grandson—after the cooking and laundry were done—I would turn off the artificial lights in the room and hold this beautiful new life in my arms for hours. I knew he would have slept just as soundly in his cradle, but I couldn't resist the pure pleasure of holding him close, of basking in that sacred light. The longer I looked, the more that light revealed.

In that light I saw his father's feet and hands, only smaller; his mother's eyes and cheeks, all in miniature. Everyone who looked saw another family member reflected in one of his features. Then, when I least expected it, I noticed something surprisingly familiar. There, when his lips moved, were my own father's mouth and chin.

My father died twenty-two years ago when my son was only eight years old, but I saw him at that moment in the promise of a new generation. I don't know if babies dream, but watching my grandson's face in that light, I did.

I was transported back in time to my own father's lap, to his short yet strong arms that carried me up the stairs to bed and over the waves in the ocean. He used to sing a song made popular by Maurice Chevalier, "Thank Heaven for Little Girls." I believed the song was written just for me, because my dad made me feel that it was. And in my grandson's face I saw my dad for the first time in many years.

We have a name for when day fades into night, and a name for when night just opens into day. We call the light that is neither day nor night *dusk* and *dawn*. These are the delicate boundaries, neither dark nor bright, where one time blends into the other. We also have a name for the light that is neither sun nor moon, where one generation folds into another. That spark of primordial light is called a *soul*.

And seeing my father in my grandson's face, I truly realized what a soul is and how it never dies. In that primordial light, I saw my father's love, and mine, passed through the generations to my son and now to his.

All the grandparents who stared transfixed at this amazing new human being saw something of themselves in the baby. His nose is his mother's and her mother's too, his toes definitely his dad's. He sneezes like his aunt. And although it may seem impossible that one infant could look like so many different people, it is nevertheless true. When someone asks the perennial question, who does the baby look like? I am tempted to answer, like everyone in his family—because in the glow of the light of creation's first day, he does.

Great-grandparents, grandparents—some present, others only in memory—were there in this child. And that is why when he closed his eyes, when he turned his head, when his mouth formed a smile, you could see a bit of the past being reborn, of one generation opening into another.

I know that birth is a biological event and that similarities in appearance are attributable to genetic inheritance, but that is not all that is true. A soul is not created out of nothing. It grows out of the hidden light of old souls, and you can see them in the face of each newborn child. To see this and to know it for the miracle that it is, is to discover where that first light is hidden and to witness creation being renewed. It is to achieve the skill sought after by the great Hasidic teacher Rabbi Nachman of Breslov, of dancing while standing still.

Midrash lets us glimpse the light of old souls who saw the glow of the holy in the words of Scripture. It invites us to find that light within our own souls and bring it to illumine the sacred narratives.

Midrash allows us to dance while standing still.

ACKNOWLEDGMENTS

Many people have made *Midrash* possible. Jon Sweeney always believed that this was a book I should write. His gentle and persistent encouragement helped me put on paper the words of midrash that I have loved and taught. I have been blessed by his fine editorial skills and his friendship. I am also grateful to Robert Edmonson for his keen eye for textual detail and clarity, which have been invaluable in the final stages of this book.

My husband, Dennis Sasso, has been not only a constant support through the many months I worked on this project, but also a faithful reader of its pages. His knowledge, his precise sense of language, and his wisdom are in this book. I am deeply grateful for the many hours he patiently looked over the manuscript with me. *His banner of love was over me* (Song of Songs 2:4).

I am thankful for the computer knowledge of Sharon Hein, who taught me new word processing skills and, when I lost patience, simply and without complaint entered many editorial changes for me.

I am honored that Joan Chittister has written the Afterword. She is an eloquent witness to the life of the spirit and speaks powerfully to all generations.

My children, David and Debbie and now also Dana and Brad, have allowed these stories to enter their lives, and their lives and loves are in these stories.

This book is dedicated to my grandson, Darwin. He is not yet old enough to speak, but his laughter and his smile are God's echo. With great anticipation I look forward to the privilege of hearing how the words of Torah are still speaking to him and making music in his soul.

Collections of Midrash in English

Bialik, Hayim Nahman, and Yehoshua Hana Ravnitzky. *The Book of Legends: Sefer Ha-Aggada.* New York: Schocken Books, 1992.

Ginzberg, Louis. *Legends of the Bible.* Philadelphia: Jewish Publication Society of America, 1975. A one-volume compendium of his seven-volume collection of midrashim.

Glatzer, Nahum N. *Hammer on the Rock: A Midrash Reader.* New York: Schocken Books, 1975.

Learning More About Midrash

Holtz, Barry W. *Back to the Sources: Reading the Classic Jewish Texts.* New York: Summit Books, 1984.

Schwartz, Howard. *Reimagining the Bible: The Storytelling of the Rabbis.* New York: Oxford University Press, 1998.

Visotzky, Burton L. *Reading the Book: Making the Bible a Timeless Text.* New York: Schocken Books, 1991.

Women's Midrash

Frankel, Ellen. *The Five Books of Miriam: A Woman's Commentary on the Torah.* San Francisco: Harper, 1998.

Hyman, Naomi M. *Biblical Women in the Midrash: A Source Book*. Northvale, NJ: Jason Aronson, 1997.

Sasso, Sandy. *But God Remembered: Stories of Women from Creation to the Promised Land*. Woodstock, VT: Jewish Lights, 1995.

Midrashic Novels

Diamant, Anita. *The Red Tent*. New York: St. Martins Press, 1997.

DuNour, Shlomo. *Adiel*. London: Toby Press, 2002.

Children's Midrash

Golden, Barbara. *A Child's Book of Midrash*. Northvale, NJ: Jason Aronson, 1990.

Lester, Julius. *When the Beginning Began: Stories About God, the Creatures and Us*. San Diego: (Harcourt Brace and Company) Silver Whistle, 1999.

Sasso, Sandy. *Adam & Eve's First Sunset: God's New Day*. Woodstock, VT: Jewish Lights, 2003.

————. *Cain and Abel: Finding the Fruits of Peace*. Woodstock, VT: Jewish Lights, 2001.

————. *Noah's Wife: The Story of Naamah*. Woodstock, VT: Jewish Lights, 1996.

Definitions of Possibly Unfamiliar Words

Akeda—the binding of Isaac, the Hebrew term for the narrative of Genesis 22

Akiba—second-century Palestinian rabbinic sage

Challah—traditional braided bread for the Sabbath meal

Decalogue—Greek designation for the Ten Commandments

Hasidism—popular mystical movement originating in eighteenth-century Eastern Europe

Ketuvim—"Writings," the third section of the traditional division of the Hebrew Bible

Kiddush—prayer of blessing over the wine for the sanctification of the Sabbath

L'chaim—customary Jewish toast, meaning "to life"

Midrash Aggadah—rabbinic interpretation of the Bible of non-legal or narrative nature

Midrash Halacha—rabbinic interpretation of the Bible yielding legal or prescriptive teachings

Mount Horeb—name for the biblical mountain where Moses has the revelation at the burning bush. It is often associated with Mount Sinai.

Mount Moriah—biblical mountain on which the binding of Isaac takes place

Mount Sinai—biblical mountain of revelation where Moses and the Israelites receive the Ten Commandments (Decalogue)

Nevi'im—"Prophets," the second section of the traditional division of the Hebrew Bible

Pardes—acronym for the four methods of rabbinic interpretation meaning "orchard" or "paradise":

peshat—meaning "simple"; literal method of rabbinic interpretation

remez—meaning "hint"; allegorical method of rabbinic interpretation

drash—meaning "search"; homiletical method of rabbinic interpretation

sod—meaning "secret" or "hidden"; mystical method of rabbinic interpretation

Pharisees—second-Temple-period group of Jewish scholars advocating oral interpretation of the Torah, who are precursors to the rabbinic tradition

Rabbi—honorific title for Jewish sage originating during the early centuries of the common era

Rosh Hashanah—the Jewish New Year occurring in the fall

Shabbat—the seventh day of the week dedicated to rest and the pursuit of holiness

Synagogue—Greek term for a house of assembly dedicated to the purposes of worship and study

Talmud—compilation of rabbinic teaching consisting of the Mishnah and the Gemara:

Mishnah—early rabbinic commentary on the Bible from 200 BCE to 200 CE

Gemara—commentary on the Mishnah produced both in the land of Israel and Babylonia from the third to the sixth centuries CE

TaNaKh—acronym for the tripartite division of the Hebrew Bible: Torah (teaching), Nevi'im (Prophets), and Ketuvim (Writings)

Temple—sacred site of sacrifice and worship in Jerusalem:

The first Temple was built by Solomon in the tenth century BCE and destroyed by the Babylonians in the sixth century BCE. The second Temple period begins with the return of the exiles from Babylonia under Ezra and Nehemiah (fifth century BCE). It was rebuilt by Herod in its grandeur in the first century BCE and destroyed by the Romans in the year 70 CE.

Torah—"teaching," specifically referring to the first five books of the Bible and more generally to the entirety of the scared tradition of Judaism:

Written Torah—the Scriptures contained in the first five books of the Bible—Genesis, Exodus, Leviticus, Numbers, and Deuteronomy

Oral Torah—the rabbinic teaching parallel to the

written text that is viewed as a continual unfolding of revelation

Tractate—name for one of the sixty-three divisions of the Mishnah

Yavneh (Jamnia)—the city outside of Jerusalem where Rabbi Yohanan ben Zakkai established a rabbinical academy following the destruction of the second Temple by the Romans

"Dear young sisters," our Scholastic director said, leaning toward us down the novitiate table, her face intense, her hands open, as if she were drawing us all into the center of them, "Remember this: the empty vessel must be filled. . . . The empty vessel must be filled."

She said the same thing year after year, conference after conference. And well she did. It took years, but I finally came to realize the implications of what she meant. Unless we ourselves were steeped in the Scriptures, no matter how sincere our work, we had nothing of any lasting value to give anyone else. And she was right. One thing I knew for sure when I finished reading this book: She would have understood *Midrash*. She would have liked it. She did, after all, spend her entire life trying to do for us what Rabbi Sasso is also trying to do in this book. "Taste and see that the Lord is sweet," the psalmist says. My formation director and Rabbi Sasso are saying the same thing.

It is the kind of thing that stands to change our entire lives.

As young Benedictine women monastics, we came from a contemplative tradition that was steeped in both the Hebrew and the Christian Scriptures. We prayed the psalms and read segments from both Scriptures at least five times a day. "Lectio Divina," Sacred Reading, was the centerpiece of the spiritual life. The formation made that clear.

Every young novice spent then and spends now hours every day on spiritual reading. We learned to read Scripture slowly. We learned to think about it. We learned to contend and contest with every major word of it. What was faith? Would we have done what Mordechai did? What did Jesus mean when he said, "Render to Caesar the things that are Caesar's and to God the things that are God's"?

We became part of the stories, challenging every idea, challenging ourselves as a result of them.

It was a long, slow process, but our ancestors, the monastics of the desert, themselves part of the early centuries in which the Torah and Rabbinic Judaism were becoming the centerpiece of Jewish life, were also more steeped in the Word than in ritual, more intent on the text itself than on either doctrine or dogmas. Their teachings on the role and value of immersion in the Scriptures were unending, unyielding. This, they taught, was the essence of the spiritual life. All things else were indeed, in the words of Rabbi Hillel, "only commentary."

Abba Poemen said: *The nature of water is yielding and that of a stone is hard. Yet, if you hang a bottle filled with water above the stone so that the water drips drop by drop, it will wear a hole in the stone. In the same way, the word of God is tender and our heart is hard. So when people hear the word of God frequently, their hearts are opened to the fear of God.*

The process is a simple one. Listen to the Word and become it in your own life, here and now.

This book is saying the same. But more than that, it comes with layers of information and insight that can change for the better the way we all look at Scripture. Not as magic but as spiritual meaning for our own times. Not as mystery but as a new and real presence in our own lives.

This book is as much about us and our lives as it is about the historical nature of midrash. By allowing us to see the connections between the reading of Scripture and the development of her own spiritual life, Rabbi Sasso gives us all the courage to do the same. She takes Scripture out of the realm of professional religionists and gives it back to those for whom it is intended. She gives it to all of us here at the foot of Sinai and asks us to listen to what God may be saying to us. Now and here.

In *Midrash* Rabbi Sasso not only shows the reader how to listen, she also makes the dialogue a living one. She makes the Scripture a living voice, one that speaks now, to us, and to us for all time. In every different condition of our lives, she shows us that the same Word may say very different things: the very things we need to know from one year to another. This God is not a static God. This God goes with us everywhere, in every situation in life. Exodus is both a challenge to faith and a moment of depression. We know that's possible because we have gone through both, and often at the same time.

Most of all, *Midrash* makes religion the realm of adult development, not the pablum, the fairy tale land, of children. This is a God good for the long haul. This God who has Abraham do something beneath him as a human being in order to prove he is a human being worth coming into contact with, is worth challenging. More, the challenge itself is required for the growth. There is no one answer for all time. There is only this one God for all time. And this God is trustworthy, understands us, is with us in everything.

Finally, *Midrash* is about freeing people to think, to themselves wrestle with God, to cross their own Red Seas, to struggle with principle over pharaonic power, however wedded we may be to it.

This book makes meaningful midrash the bridge between us and the God we seek. It fills us up with God. It gives us something worthwhile to give to everyone else.

"God enters a private door into every individual," Emerson wrote. No doubt about it. The entering is what seeds us for life. The seeding changes us as well as grows us. The seed of God is what we become. The mystic Meister Eckhart makes it clear. He writes: "The seed of God is in us all. Pear seeds grow into pear trees, nut seeds into nut trees, and God-seed into God."

This is a book about filling ourselves with the seed that is God. It is not a book to be taken lightly. You see, my Scholastic director knew it, too. "The empty vessel must be filled," she taught us. "The empty vessel must be filled."

JOAN CHITTISTER, OSB

NOTES

1. Martin Buber, *Ten Rungs: Hasidic Sayings* (New York: Schocken Books, 1965), 59–60.

2. Burton Visotzky, *Reading the Book: Making the Bible a Timeless Text* (New York: Schocken Books, 1991),4.

3. Robert Alter, *The Art of Biblical Narrative:* (New York: Basic Books, 1981), 189.

4. Raymond E. Brown, *An Introduction to the New Testament* (New York: Doubleday, 1997), 34, 45.

5. Jeffrey Rubenstein, *Talmudic Stories: Narrative Art, Composition and Culture* (Baltimore: John Hopkins University Press, 1999), 282.

6. Barry W. Holtz, *Back to the Sources: Reading the Classic Jewish Texts* (New York: Summit Books, 1984), 193.

7. Ibid., 194–97.

8. Abraham Joshua Heschel, "The Moral Outrage of Vietnam" in *Vietnam: Crisis of Conscience*, edited by Robert McAfee Brown, Abraham Joshua Heschel and Michael Novak (New York: Association Press, Behrman House and Hardert Herder, 1967), 51–52.

9. Shalom Spiegel, *The Last Trial* (Woodstock,VT: Jewish Lights, 1993), 5.

10. Ibid., 6.

ABOUT PARACLETE PRESS

WHO WE ARE

Paraclete Press is a publisher of books, recordings, and DVDs on Christian spirituality. Our publishing represents a full expression of Christian belief and practice—from Catholic to Evangelical, from Protestant to Orthodox.

We are the publishing arm of the Community of Jesus, an ecumenical monastic community in the Benedictine tradition. As such, we are uniquely positioned in the marketplace without connection to a large corporation and with informal relationships to many branches and denominations of faith.

WHAT WE ARE DOING

PARACLETE PRESS BOOKS | Paraclete publishes books that show the richness and depth of what it means to be Christian. Although Benedictine spirituality is at the heart of who we are and all that we do, we publish books that reflect the Christian experience across many cultures, time periods, and houses of worship. We publish books that nourish the vibrant life of the church and its people.

We have several different series, including the bestselling Paraclete Essentials and Paraclete Giants series of classic texts in contemporary English; Voices from the Monastery—men and women monastics writing about living a spiritual life today; our award-winning Paraclete Poetry series as well as the Mount Tabor Books on the arts; bestselling gift books for children on the occasions of baptism and first communion; and the Active Prayer Series that brings creativity and liveliness to any life of prayer.

MOUNT TABOR BOOKS | Paraclete's newest series, Mount Tabor Books, focuses on the arts and literature as well as liturgical worship and spirituality, and was created in conjunction with the Mount Tabor Ecumenical Centre for Art and Spirituality in Barga, Italy.

PARACLETE RECORDINGS | From Gregorian chant to contemporary American choral works, our recordings celebrate the best of sacred choral music composed through the centuries that create a space for heaven and earth to intersect. Paraclete Recordings is the record label representing the internationally acclaimed choir Gloriæ Dei Cantores, praised for their "rapt and fathomless spiritual intensity" by *American Record Guide;* the Gloriæ Dei Cantores Schola, specializing in the study and performance of Gregorian chant; and the other instrumental artists of the Arts Empowering Life Foundation.

Paraclete Press is also privileged to be the exclusive North American distributor of the recordings of the Monastic Choir of St. Peter's Abbey in Solesmes, France, long considered to be a leading authority on Gregorian chant.

PARACLETE VIDEO | Our DVDs offer spiritual help, healing, and biblical guidance for a broad range of life issues including grief and loss, marriage, forgiveness, facing death, bullying, addictions, Alzheimer's, and spiritual formation.

Learn more about us at our website:
www.paracletepress.com or phone us
toll-free at 1.800.451.5006

 SCAN TO READ MORE

You may also be interested in …

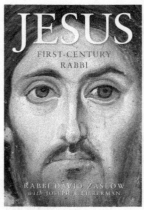

JESUS
First-Century Rabbi
Rabbi David Zaslow
with Joseph Lieberman

ISBN 978-1-61261-644-5
Paperback
$16.99

This bold, fresh look at the historical Jesus and the Jewish roots of Christianity challenges both Jews and Christians to re-examine their understanding of Jesus and his commitment to his Jewish faith. Instead of emphasizing the differences between the two religions, this groundbreaking text explains how the concepts of vicarious atonement, mediation, incarnation, and Trinity are actually rooted in classical Judaism. Using the cutting edge of scholarly research, Rabbi Zaslow dispels the myths of disparity between Christianity and Judaism without diluting the unique features of each. *Jesus: First-Century Rabbi* is a breath of fresh air for Christians and Jews who want to understand one another, as well as strengthen and deepen their own faith traditions.

Rabbi David Zaslow is the spiritual leader of Havurah Shir Hadash, a synagogue in Ashland, Oregon, and one of the foremost leaders in the Jewish Renewal movement. He is the editor of the bestselling Hebrew/English prayerbook, *Ivdu Et Hashem B'Simcha* ("Serve the Holy One With Joy"). Rabbi Zaslow travels the country leading workshops with churches and synagogues on the Jewish roots of Christianity.

CPSIA information can be obtained
at www.ICGtesting.com
Printed in the USA
BVHW080955171121
621844BV00006B/92